RUTH

loss, love & legacy

KELLY MINTER

Lifeway Press®
Brentwood, Tennessee

**EDITORIAL TEAM,
LIFEWAY WOMEN
BIBLE STUDIES**

Becky Loyd
Director,
Lifeway Women

Tina Boesch
Manager

Chelsea Waack
Production Leader

Laura Magness
Content Editor

Erin Franklin
Production Editor

Lauren Ervin
Graphic Designer

Published by Lifeway Press® • © 2022 Kelly Minter

ISBN: 978-1-0877-4948-8
Item: 005833829
Dewey decimal classification: 222.35
Subject heading: BIBLE. O.T. RUTH \ CHRISTIAN LIFE \ FAITH

To order additional copies of this resource, write Lifeway Resources Customer Service; 200 Powell Place, Suite 100, Brentwood, TN, 37027-7707; FAX order to 615.251.5933; call toll-free 800.458.2772; email orderentry@lifeway.com; or order online at lifeway.com.

Printed in the United States of America

Lifeway Women Bible Studies
Lifeway Resources
200 Powell Place, Suite 100
Brentwood, TN, 37027-7707

CONTENTS

ABOUT THE AUTHOR

KELLY MINTER is passionate about God's Word and believes it permeates all of life. The personal healing and steadfast hope she's found in the pages of Scripture fuels her passion to connect God's Word to our everyday lives. When she's not writing or teaching, you can find her tending her garden, taking a walk with friends, cooking for her nieces and nephews, riding a boat down the Amazon River, or walking through a Moldovan village with Justice & Mercy International.

Kelly's past Bible studies include *Encountering God: Cultivating Habits of Faith through the Spiritual Disciplines*; *Finding God Faithful: A Study on the Life of Joseph*; *No Other Gods: The Unrivaled Pursuit of Christ*; *All Things New: A Study on 2 Corinthians*; *What Love Is: The Letters of 1, 2 & 3 John*; and *Nehemiah: A Heart That Can Break*.

Kelly partners with Justice & Mercy International (JMI), an organization that cares for the vulnerable and forgotten with the love of Jesus in the Amazon and Moldova. To find out more about JMI, visit justiceandmercy.org/cultivate. And to learn more about Kelly's Bible studies, books, music, and speaking schedule, visit kellyminter.com.

WHAT'S INSIDE

Personal Study Each week you'll have five days of personal study. I'll walk you verse-by-verse through the book of Ruth, with questions to help you process and apply what you read. After you finish a week of personal study, it's time to watch the teaching video.

Watch These pages provide a place to take notes from the video teachings. You'll want to begin your study with the Session One video and then watch the rest of the videos after you finish each week of personal study.

Recipes I've included some of my favorite recipes for you to enjoy over the next seven sessions you spend studying Ruth. Make these together with your Bible study group, friends, or family, or enjoy them on your own!

LEADING A GROUP?

Whether a large or small group, we have what you need to lead women through *Ruth*. Visit **lifeway.com/ruth** for free leader downloads, including a Leader Guide PDF, promotional resources, and more.

STUDY QUESTIONS

In each day of study, you'll find a mix of basic observation questions along with the following types of questions that help you dig deeper in your study:

PERSONAL TAKE questions invite you to record your thoughts on the meaning of the Scripture passage being studied. Sometimes these questions have no right or wrong answers but require you to consider why you lean in a certain direction.

PERSONAL REFLECTION is a time to reflect on what you're learning—about God and yourself. These questions will challenge you to consider how what you're learning reminds you of who God is, impacts the way you see Him, shapes your character, and makes you more like Christ.

PERSONAL RESPONSE questions challenge you to take an action to apply or respond to what you're learning.

SESSION 1
INTRODUCTION

The book of Ruth, nestled in the Old Testament between Judges and 1 Samuel, is a short, four-chapter narrative that bundles the human experience of loss, love, and legacy with the divine hope and sovereignty of a redeeming God. From its pages steps a wayfaring foreigner into the town of Bethlehem, amidst hardship and famine and tragedy, affecting the course of human history forever.

A widow turned wife, a servant turned heir, a childless foreigner turned mother, she was born in Moab but found her home in Israel. Ruth. The name that chimes a thousand redeeming notes for every woman who has ever been devastated by loss, struggled as a stranger, lived with the bitter, longed to be loved, fought for crumbs, or wept along the journey. She is an emblem of grace for every flawed and ailing sinner who has lived in her wake, not because of her own nobility but because of the One under whose wings she came to trust—the God of Israel.

Despite heartbreak and trial, Ruth is an accessible image of integrity, kindness, purity, commitment, faith, and hard work as a marginalized outsider and vulnerable widow.

Ruth's story runs the gamut of human experience, inviting us to engage with God about our own stories. Despite heartbreak and trial, she is an accessible image of integrity, kindness, purity, commitment, faith, and hard work as a marginalized outsider and vulnerable widow. She is godliness with its sleeves rolled up. Perhaps most impressive, she is a committed God-fearer despite profound loss and with a mother-in-law who changed her name to Mara, which incidentally means "bitter." (I think this means they weren't baking a lot of cookies together. Or sharing sweaters.)

When I first wrote about Ruth and the book that bears her name, I was in my early thirties, single, and exiting not the land of Moab but the music industry, so kind of the same. It was a time in life when I particularly related to Ruth's aloneness, feeling like an outsider, longing for that one person to choose me. I wrestled with her resolve to follow God when by all accounts it appeared He had let her down, or at the very least let down the mother-in-law she lived with. As I write today, I am still single though not unhappy. I have found God enduringly faithful even when I don't understand Him. And when I think of the book of Ruth, I don't only think of Ruth, Boaz, or Naomi but the redemption of Jesus Christ under whose wings each of us, no matter our past, is invited to take refuge.

It is one of my prayers that this study results in you loving Jesus more deeply. The whole book yearns forward toward Him. And if you're studying with others, I'm expectant for the fellowship you will experience that comes uniquely by being in God's Word together. You are not alone. Ruth and her God await you.

Kelly Minter

WATCH

WATCH the Session One video teaching and take notes below.

#RUTHSTUDY

LEADING A GROUP?

Don't miss the free Leader Guide PDF, group promotional resources, and more at **lifeway.com/ruth**

YOU'LL FIND DETAILED INFORMATION FOR HOW TO **ACCESS THE VIDEO SESSIONS** THAT ACCOMPANY THIS STUDY ON THE CARD INSERTED IN THE BACK OF YOUR BIBLE STUDY BOOK.

9

SESSION 2
TWO
JOURNEYS

In the early part of 2008, I began work on *Ruth*, my first verse-by-verse Bible study. More recently, it has been a pleasure to set my hand to updating and revising that original manuscript. Almost everything needs an occasional update. Think of how many iterations blue jeans go through in just a decade. For certain, the Bible never needs to *get with the times*, but as God's Word has continued to change me, so I wanted to bring to bear those revelations, that maturity, to this Bible study that is so dear to my heart.

I wonder if you've ever read through old diaries, cringing as you reminisce. *Why did I make such a big deal about that? Please tell me I never thought that!* Oh, the drama. And then in the same sitting, maybe on the same page, you come across some beautiful gem of wisdom, a piece of insight you didn't even think you were smart enough to possess, much less pen. Welcome to the life of an author. You go back and read across old works, a little embarrassed at certain points and a tiny bit wowed at others. This was certainly the case as I read back through *Ruth*.

If there's something that deserved more focus in this edition, it's the greater story in which Ruth's story sits. If the four chapters of Ruth were the only part of the Bible you'd ever read, you might get the impression that Ruth and Boaz were something of the world's original model citizens we'd all do our best to emulate. You might conclude that if you can just be more like them with a New Testament spin, you'll be a better Christian than when you first started. This is not completely wrong, but it misses the much larger story in which Ruth and Boaz are a part.

> The Bible never needs to *get with the times*, but as God's Word has continued to change me, so I wanted to bring to bear those revelations, that maturity, to this Bible study that is so dear to my heart.

So, we'll keep an eye out for how the book of Ruth shines light on the greater whole of the Bible, and vice versa. We'll better understand where the book of Ruth sits within the narrative of the Old Testament. And we'll discover some of the prophetic ways the characters, and God's providence and provision, all point forward to ultimate redemption in Christ. We'll still fall in love with Ruth and Boaz because they're positively lovable people who have much to teach us. But we'll never take our eyes off the bigger story—God's grand drama of redemption.

If you don't already have some of this contextual knowledge, don't you worry one second. We'll do this together. But some of you have a lot of preexisting Bible knowledge. If this is the case, let me encourage you to explore. If you see a cross-reference in your Bible, chase it; if a verse tugs at your heart, pause and refresh yourself from its well. Everyone has permission to dig, scrape, investigate, and go beyond the borders of these pages. You're sure to discover wonderful insights—ones I've never thought of.

Lastly, and this is a big one, be looking not just for the practical portrayals of character qualities—love, generosity, faith, tenacity, courage, kindness, self-sacrifice, obedience—but also for what these reveal about the heart and nature of God. It's easy for us Bible students, us list-checker-off-ers, to try to better ourselves by implementing the tangible qualities we see in people like Ruth, Boaz, and, at times, Naomi. As we should! I can't imagine what rails I would have sailed over if not for godly examples of what being a serious follower of Christ looks like. At the same time, if we focus solely on behavioral changes and not on who God is throughout the story, we'll turn ourselves into well-groomed rule followers who appear holy on the outside but have little love or grace or dependence on Christ. And we don't want that, I know. So, we'll always, always keep our eyes open for the redemptive nature and work of God. Because if I've learned anything between the first and second writing, it's that His grace is everything.

YOUR GOD WILL BE MY GOD.

Ruth 1:16

DAY 1
FLEEING HOME

The book
of Ruth is
prophetic in
many respects.
There is a
story behind
the story.

My first memorable encounter with the book of Ruth took place in the hunter green pews of Reston Bible Church—the church my dad and mom founded a year before I was born. We were there to hear a visiting speaker. The borderline gruff, elderly Englishman named Major Ian Thomas taught through the book of Ruth for almost two hours. I was captivated, which says a lot for a twelve-year-old who would have preferred being somewhere else on a Friday night. I remember Major Thomas exposing the fascinating symbolism that runs throughout Ruth as if he were tugging on a camouflaged thread with the skill of a seamstress.

The book of Ruth is prophetic in many respects. There is a story behind the story. Listening to Major Thomas is the first time I recall being taught the Old Testament Scriptures with the New Testament so compellingly in view. He is the one who helped me see the hints of Jesus woven throughout this short book. (I also remember him being distinctly against hats in the sanctuary, so make what you will of what has stuck with me.) This man of faith has since gone on to be with the Lord, but I am grateful to remember him as someone who kindled a love in my heart for the person of Ruth and, more importantly, her God.

Today I'm anxious to begin surveying the historical context and setting of this short but powerful book with you. It will be like pulling back the shades of your hotel room and remembering you're in New York City. This means world-class shows, coffee, and pizza are at hand. Context tells us a lot.

CAREFULLY READ RUTH 1:1-2. Elimelech's family lived in Bethlehem-Judah, and they were called

_____ .

To be an Ephrathite meant to be from Bethlehem-Judah, which was also known as Ephrathah. Since Bethlehem was in ancient Israel, Elimelech's family were also considered Israelites. (Sort of like being a New Yorker also means you're an American.)

Why did Elimelech and Naomi leave Bethlehem-Judah for Moab? Circle your answer.

There was a famine in Bethlehem.   They had relatives in Moab.

There was a war in Bethlehem.   A judge ordered them to leave.

READ GENESIS 19:30-38. What do these verses say about the origin of the Moabites?

Next to each passage, describe the relationship between the Israelites and the Moabites.

Deuteronomy 23:3-6

Judges 3:12-14

Understanding the history of Moab and her relationship with Israel changes the tone of Elimelech and Naomi's journey. It wasn't as if they were Americans slipping into Canada for a spell. Moab was an enemy of Israel. The Moabites' blatant idolatry was a sure sign that the Israelites were to remain separate. The author of Ruth doesn't explicitly tell us how to feel about Elimelech's decision to move his family, but we know from Deuteronomy 30:1-9 that God promised to restore His people when they returned to Him in obedience. We also know that Bethlehem was God's chosen place for His people. So as scholar Daniel I. Block notes, "It seems, however, that Elimelech designed his own solution instead of calling on God for mercy and repenting of the sins that plagued the nation during the dark days of the judges."[1]

After the Lord freed the Israelites from the land of Egypt, they wandered in the desert for forty years. They lived as vagabonds, their tents pulled up and pinned down over and over like finicky campers. Then one day Joshua led them across the Jordan River into Canaan, the land of promise that flowed with milk and honey and, more importantly, with permanence. God had given them a home; they didn't need to look anywhere else.

The city of Bethlehem, where Elimelech's family lived, was a hill country in the land of Judah and part of the promised land of Canaan. Ironically, Bethlehem means "House of Bread," and there hadn't been much of that since their departure. You may be thinking, *If God had given the Israelites a permanent place to live where He promised to take care of them, why the famine?*

> **READ JUDGES 2:11-19.** What did God's people often do when a judge died (v. 19)?

> **PERSONAL TAKE:** What evidence do you see for why there was a famine in the land?

> Now look back at Ruth 1:1 and fill in the blank using the Christian Standard Bible (CSB) translation: "During the time of the _____, there was a famine in the land."

The story of Ruth took place during the time of the Judges, a period of approximately 450 years when God raised up different governors to rule and guide Israel. This period stretched from the time Joshua led the Israelites into the promised land to King Saul being crowned the first king of Israel. A quick skim through the book of Judges reveals that God's people had a history of turning to Him during seasons of turmoil but forgetting Him during seasons of prosperity.

> **PERSONAL REFLECTION:** Are you currently in a season of trial, blessing, or both? How are your current circumstances negatively or positively affecting your relationship with God?

Perhaps you've thought or heard it said that theology isn't all that important; what matters is your relationship with God. But what we believe about God (our theology) impacts our relationship with Him. If we believe that difficult circumstances are a sign of God's cruelty, indifference, or displeasure with us, how deeply does that affect our intimacy with Him? On the other hand, thinking that God is happy with us only when everything is going our way is equally detrimental to our faith. We'll see in our study together that it is His presence with us that is superior to our circumstances, no matter how trying or wonderful.

Let's close by drawing Elimelech and Naomi's plight back to our own. They stood on the precipice of two compelling choices—stay in the arid land of God's choosing or flee to the bountiful one God had forbidden. We know that Elimelech chose the latter. The question for us is: *What will we choose?* Perhaps the loneliness is unbearable, your heartache is unrelenting, or a daily burden has become overwhelming. The attractive land of Moab is calling, but you know it represents compromises of all sorts. When we're weary in obedience, escaping to easier terrain is tempting, but it always comes at a cost.

READ GALATIANS 6:9. What did Paul say will happen if we don't give up in doing good?

READ HEBREWS 11:24-26. What did Moses regard as of greater value than the treasures of Egypt? And to what was he looking ahead?

PERSONAL REFLECTION: How do these verses encourage you to stand firm where God has you? Be thoughtful about your response.

The late Matthew Henry astutely points out that fleeing our circumstances doesn't necessarily remedy them. "It is our wisdom to make the best of that which is, for it is seldom that changing our place is mending it."[2] No matter how many times I read that quote, it always feels like a word. How often do I want my circumstances to change when really God wants to change me? God is present right where you are. Stay put and stand firm. It is always more blessed to be in the fellowship of His presence than anywhere else.

DAY 2
RETURNING HOME

The first chapter of Ruth is a story of two journeys.

The first chapter of Ruth is a story of two journeys: the journey from Bethlehem to Moab and the journey from Moab back to Bethlehem. The first is briefly described in the two verses we studied yesterday, but the second journey, the journey of return, takes the rest of the chapter.

BEFORE LOOKING AT TODAY'S READING, REREAD RUTH 1:1-2.

Name the four people who traveled from Bethlehem to Moab.

To refresh your memory, all four family members were from Bethlehem and were called what? Circle your answer.

Bethlehemites   Canaanites   Ephrathites   Amorites

They were from the town of Bethlehem and the nation of _____. (See p. 14 if you need help.)

NOW THAT WE HAVE THESE DETAILS, READ VERSES 3-7 TWO TIMES AT A REFLECTIVE PACE. Take a moment to appreciate the gravity of these tragic circumstances.

One of the most significant differences between the journey from Bethlehem to Moab and the journey from Moab back to Bethlehem is the difference in people. Naomi was the only one to take both journeys. Though she left with two sons and a husband, she returned with two women who were not her flesh and blood.

Below, write the names of Naomi's daughters-in-law, their nationality, and the name of the son each of them married. (See 4:10 for whom Ruth and Orpah were married to.)

Name	Nationality	Married To

READ DEUTERONOMY 7:3-4 AND 1 KINGS 11:1-4. Why could it have been problematic for Mahlon and Chilion to marry Moabite women?

In Deuteronomy 7:1-8, the Lord commanded the people of Israel not to intermarry with certain nations. The events of 1 Kings 11 took place after the events in Ruth, but they give us a good picture of why entering into a covenant relationship with these nations was problematic. Solomon's heart was led astray to other gods because of his marriages to women from nations that didn't worship the one true God. Solomon could not be fully devoted to the Lord and devoted to the gods of other nations.

It deserves special attention that God's warnings had nothing to do with certain races; rather, He warned against His people aligning with nations that had rejected Him. For a New Testament perspective on this, read 2 Corinthians 6:14-18.

PERSONAL TAKE: What reasoning did Paul use to encourage separation between Christians and non-Christians when it comes to deep covenantal bonds?

The apostle Paul instructed Christians not to be "yoked together" (or deeply tied) to unbelievers because the life-paths of each party will naturally move in opposite directions (v. 14). We are called to love and reach out to all people, but when we attach ourselves through covenant bonds to those who don't follow Christ, our love for Him will eventually be compromised. (This principle—which we see in action in Ruth, Deuteronomy, 1 Kings, and 2 Corinthians—will be of even greater significance to us in the coming days.)

Why did Naomi decide to return to Bethlehem (Ruth 1:6-7)?

PERSONAL RESPONSE: Have you ever turned back to God out of desperation or necessity? If so, describe it here.

God's ways are not always the most practical, popular, or unopposed, but they are the most blessed.

A desire for physical nourishment caused Naomi to leave Moab; this same desire would lead her back. The catalyst behind both journeys appears to be governed by the physical, not so much the spiritual, though I imagine the spiritual losses—fellowship, worship, residing in the land—were in view all along the way. Our physical circumstances are vital, and we should always take them into account. But I suppose the question is: *What ultimately dictates our decisions—our circumstances or the God of them?*

The challenge of staying committed to God when times are tough and seemingly greener pastures are a mere fence-hop away is one I know. Feel-good remedies abound for the loneliness and challenges of singleness. Clinging to Christ and His promise of company and provision instead of reaching for the many available tonics has been an exercise I have both failed and succeeded at. His grace has held me fast even when my choices have looked more like Elimelech and Naomi's. This I know for sure: God's ways are not always the most practical, popular, or unopposed, but they are the most blessed. But I don't want us to get too far ahead of ourselves.

PERSONAL RESPONSE: Think about a time when you allowed your circumstances to direct you instead of leaving room for God's direction. How did this cause you to more quickly act on God's leading in the future?

LOOK BACK AT VERSE 6. From where did Naomi hear that God had come to the aid of His people? What about this feels significant?

I will never get over this. It was within the dark and dreaded land of Moab, the land of her family's choosing, that Naomi heard of God's provision. The echoes of His mercy somehow reached her ears in a place where God wasn't supposed to be heard, in a land God's goodness wasn't supposed to reach.

PERSONAL RESPONSE: Briefly write about a time when God pursued you—even drew you back—when you were in a far-off place. What did you discover about His nature through that experience?

I've spent time in the distant land of my choosing, haunted by the warm glow of God's provision that seemed to be for everyone else but me. I pouted against Him in my disobedience, angry I wasn't experiencing Him but not wanting to change my allegiances either. I will never stop giving Him thanks for coming for me, even against what I wanted at the time. I wonder if Naomi would later feel similarly. Her return to Bethlehem wasn't necessarily out of a longing for her God but for His provision. God spread His table for her regardless. We will discover in this story that He is as generous with grace as He is with grain.

PERSONAL TAKE: I can understand why Naomi decided to return to her homeland when she learned the famine had passed, but why do you think Ruth and Orpah decided to go with her? Naomi's family moved to a foreign country out of need, but what might Ruth and Orpah's reasons have been?

When Naomi heard that God had come to help her people in Bethlehem, she and her daughters-in-law prepared to return home (v. 6). The word *return* is a key theme of this chapter, a word that reminds us it's never too late to come home. The God of grace was welcoming Naomi back to where she belonged, and what is more surprising is that the invitation was extended to two Moabite women. Psalm 16 feels like a fitting benediction for us as we consider the place God desires for us to dwell.

REFLECT ON PSALM 16:1-6.

PERSONAL RESPONSE: If you need to return to God in some way, write about the preparations you're willing to make. If you're in a place of peace and fellowship with Him, thank Him for His presence and provision.

No matter where you are, bread is always available at His table for anyone willing to return.

DAY 3
WEEPING FORWARD

I work closely with Justice & Mercy International (JMI), an organization that serves in the Amazon jungles of Brazil and the Eastern European country of Moldova. One of our primary ministries in Moldova is our Transitional Living Program. We have two boys and two girls' homes where teenagers from broken or abusive families come to live in a loving environment. The three-year program consists of learning life skills, studying God's Word, going to school and work, and mostly being part of a loving family environment. Despite the tragic pasts of these teenagers, many are growing into some of the finest young men and women I know, unfolding as individual flowers in morning's light. Pain has marked each of them, but what they do with their pain determines their paths forward. Those who have chosen to follow Jesus are extraordinary examples of how God can transform even our greatest hardships into blessing.

God's grace is always positioned for anyone who will simply come.

Today we find Naomi packing her bags and hitting the road back to Judah. She'll return to the place she left but not as the same person. Tragedy and loss have etched scars on her heart. She'll head back without her husband or sons, bitter at God, and with two trailing daughters-in-law she wishes would just leave her alone already because she's not in the *in-law, let's-have-tea* mood right now. This is not the way any of us envision Naomi returning, but then again, she probably never imagined it this way either. Who can blame her despairing posture? And yet, like my TL friends, what she chooses to do with her grief will make all the difference for her.

How gracious that God was already in Bethlehem waiting for her, waiting for whomever else would choose to come with her, stranger or not. Naomi just didn't know it yet. We'll see in the sessions to come that God's grace is always positioned for anyone who will simply come.

READ RUTH 1:7-14 AND SLOWLY TAKE IN THE DETAILS.

Naomi said, "May the LORD show kindness to you as you have shown to the dead and to me" (v. 8). The word *kindness* doesn't do justice to the Hebrew word it translates—hesed—a profound word throughout the book of Ruth. Consider the following descriptions of this term:

> A strong relational term that wraps up in itself an entire cluster of concepts, all the positive attributes of God—love, mercy, grace, kindness, goodness, benevolence, loyalty, covenant faithfulness: in short, that quality that moves a person to act for the benefit of another without respect to the advantage it might bring to the one who expresses it.[3]

> Israel associated [hesed] with Yahweh's covenant relationship with her . . . despite her waywardness, Yahweh always stood steadfastly by Israel in "covenant loyalty."[4]

> Love, grace, mercy, kindness—all of the positive acts of devotion that flow out of a covenantal relationship.[5]

> **Based on these definitions, distill the idea of hesed into your own words.**

PERSONAL TAKE: Given that the word was often used as a unique, covenant-love between God and Israel, how is it significant that Naomi asked God to show hesed to Ruth and Orpah?

PERSONAL REFLECTION: Who has shown you hesed? Describe the person and what he or she has done for you.

We're going to table our study of *hese̱d* for now, but we'll keep coming back to it as we study. It's a concept that is essential to God's covenant love for His people.

Before writing this Bible study, I'd read the book of Ruth many times. For some reason, I'd mistakenly thought that Naomi urged Ruth and Orpah to stay in Moab before they'd set out on their trip. This seemed logical—having the discussion before they packed all their bags, said their goodbyes, and forwarded the mail.

Where did Naomi's discussion with her daughters-in-law take place (v. 7)?

Naomi, Ruth, and Orpah packed their bags, left their homes, and had gotten somewhere down the road when Naomi started urging them to go back. I guess it's a little like being a kid on vacation, stuffed in the family station wagon, six hours from home when you start fighting with your siblings and your dad and mom promise they're not afraid to turn this car right around if everyone doesn't shape up. I don't remember how old I was when I realized that they were never going to actually do that.

What reason did Naomi first give them for returning to Moab?

In verse 10, who turned back? Circle your answer.

Ruth   Orpah   Both Ruth and Orpah   Neither

Naomi realized she had two very determined and committed in-laws on her hands. When they didn't respond to her initial nudging, she snipped the threads of their faintest hopes. *You're following me to Bethlehem because I'm your only hope for another husband. Even if I got married and pregnant with another son tonight, you'd have to wait twenty years for him to grow up. Seeing that's unlikely—and a little sketchy—you best cut me and your losses and find another husband your own age in Moab who can take care of you. Oh, and the Lord's hand has gone out against me. So, there's that.*

After Naomi's compelling argument, how did they respond (v. 14)?

One of my dear friends moved to Nashville from Boone, North Carolina. She had lived in Boone for twenty years and had made a home whose roots held almost as firm as the surrounding Appalachian Mountains. Leaving was not a consideration until the Lord opened up a tailor-made job for her in Nashville and the Holy Spirit's leading became even stronger than those mountains she awoke to every morning. Through months of tears and grief, she packed her bags, made the journey, and dug a new foundation in Tennessee. Fortunately for me, she landed about a mile down the road. My friend wept, but she wept forward.

Verse 14 reminds me that though there will be weeping in this life, the direction in which we weep is what truly matters.

> According to Ruth 1:7-14, who wept going forward and who wept going backward? Describe your answer below.

PERSONAL TAKE: Orpah kissed her mother-in-law goodbye, but Ruth clung to her. What do you think motivated each of their decisions?

This idea of weeping in different directions is something we can all relate to. In the following passages, compare and contrast both individuals in the chart. Specifically, how did their grief affect their direction?

RICH YOUNG RULER Mark 10:17-22	WOMAN AT JESUS'S FEET Luke 7:36-38,48-50

Though there will be weeping in this life, the direction in which we weep is what truly matters.

RICH YOUNG RULER Mark 10:17-22	WOMAN AT JESUS'S FEET Luke 7:36-38,48-50

The woman at Jesus's feet wept but didn't allow her grief to stop her forward motion, but the rich young man walked away from Christ with great sadness. How often we too have been tempted to turn back in the face of loss or adversity. But how great the honor and reward of Ruth and the woman at Jesus's feet who, in their tears, kept walking forward.

PERSONAL RESPONSE: Are you in a season of grief that makes you want to stop or turn around? What would weeping forward as you continue to follow Christ look like for you? If this doesn't describe your current season, write about a past experience of weeping forward and what you gained from that experience.

God sees your tears. Cry them, feel them, wipe them, but don't let them stop you from moving toward Christ. It's possible to cry and walk. We will see this truth continue to blossom into the weeks ahead.

DAY 4
A LONG OBEDIENCE

Both nature and Scripture are filled with profound discoveries for those expecting to uncover something new. Be expectant in the Lord today.

One of the nice things about the short length of the book of Ruth is that we're able to take our time. I realize we're only to verse 14 and it's taken us three days to get here, but I'm savoring the slow pace. When I walk with my four-year-old niece, Lily, we make little forward progress but ample discovery progress. She pauses to examine pebbles, twirl oak leaves, and snap twigs in two. This is the leisurely but intentional pace of thoughtful Bible reading. Both nature and Scripture are filled with profound discoveries for those expecting to uncover something new. Be expectant in the Lord today.

READ RUTH 1:15. (I was serious about slow.)

Naomi refused to abandon her In-Laws-Turn-Back campaign even after Orpah went home and Ruth clung to her side.

How many times did Naomi urge Ruth to turn back (vv. 8-15)?

Give two reasons why Naomi encouraged Ruth to go back (v. 15).

PERSONAL TAKE: Why do you think Naomi was so adamant about not having Ruth and Orpah return to Bethlehem with her?

The text doesn't tell us, but it's possible Naomi didn't want anyone to know her sons had married Moabites since they were outside the covenant nation of Israel. If she returned home alone, perhaps this would remain concealed.[6] Whatever the reason, Ruth withstood several of Naomi's discouraging appeals to turn back. Obedience to God is often met with challenges that persuade us to change our minds. I used to think obedience was a one-and-done decision, but I now realize it might mean having to make that same choice several times in a week, month, or year. Orpah made it through Naomi's first round of convincing persuasions (v. 10), but after Naomi's second and third push, Orpah gave in.

> **PERSONAL RESPONSE:** Describe a time when you obeyed in the midst of consecutive trials or temptations. What did you discover about Christ and His blessings?

Obedience to God is often met with challenges that persuade us to change our minds.

Orpah set her course toward the God of Israel, but when doubts about her security settled in, she turned back. We can all relate to wanting to run back to the familiar in the middle of hard obedience. But we can also relate to the unparalleled blessings that arrive after prolonged obedience through temptation and adversity. These long stretches are what Scripture often refers to as "testing" (Jas. 1:2-4). This word doesn't mean the grade you're hoping to get on the obedience test God just passed out; rather, it's the idea of pure metals being tested. As gold passes through a purifying flame, its nature is proven (1 Pet. 1:7). The dross is skimmed off, and the gold shows itself for what it is.

Ruth's steadfast journey toward the God of Israel is similar to an account that took place before her time. Jacob's son Joseph was sold by his brothers to an Egyptian named Potiphar. While serving faithfully in his master's house, Potiphar's wife persistently tried to seduce him.

READ GENESIS 39:1-10 AND FILL IN THE BLANK FROM VERSE 10 USING THE CSB TRANSLATION.

"Although she spoke to Joseph _____ _____ _____, he refused to go to bed with her."

I wonder how many times Joseph had to choose obedience in the face of temptation. He wouldn't have escaped her seductive trap had he only stood firm once. Instead, he had to choose righteousness day after day. Ruth and Naomi's relationship was clearly different from that of Joseph and Potiphar's wife, but Ruth still needed the resolve to move toward the God of Israel while Naomi tried to talk her out of it. At the same time, obedience to God requires more than willpower. Ruth's and Joseph's obedience wasn't based on self-determination alone; rather, their motivation was anchored in something deeper than their inner resolve.

> You'll need to glance at tomorrow's reading to answer this, but compare Joseph's statement to his master's wife (Gen. 39:9) with Ruth's statement to Naomi (Ruth 1:16-17). Whom did Joseph and Ruth both reference?

Only a love for Christ will sustain obedience to Him.

> In what way did the living God factor into their obedience?

> READ JOHN 14:15. Jesus says if we _____ Him, we'll keep His _____.

Ruth's and Joseph's commitment to obedience stemmed from their commitments to God. And as New Testament believers, our obedience flows from our love for Jesus. Only a love for Him will sustain obedience to Him.

> PERSONAL RESPONSE: Since enduring obedience hinges on our love for Jesus, take a minute to evaluate your relationship with Him. Where are you struggling to trust, love, or believe in Him? How is it affecting your resolve to follow Him?

Joseph could have succumbed to Potiphar's wife's pleas for intimacy—who would have blamed him after being sold into slavery by his brothers, seemingly abandoned by God. And Ruth could have returned to Moab with her sister-in-law, Orpah. Surely no one would have cast a stone at her for choosing the familiar over an embittered mother-in-law and a foreign people. But neither

Joseph nor Ruth was looking for easy outs or rationalizations. They'd tasted the goodness of the God of Israel, and despite opposition, their faith emerged as gold.

When we lose sight of God's goodness and holiness, we're prone to justifying decisions that oppose His Word and heart. But when we believe God is good and obeying Him is for our freedom, we will change our courses for the sake of obedience. Perhaps no one changed her course more than Ruth when she decided to leave her people, false gods, and homeland for the God of Israel.

> **PERSONAL RESPONSE:** Do you need to make a life change in order to protect your path of obedience? It can be large or small. Write about it here.

Ruth and Joseph each showed resolve as they walked out their obedience to God while doing whatever it took to preserve their obedience. In the New Testament, the book of James touches on this beautifully.

> Close by reflecting on these fitting verses as you seek to persevere in obedience. How does each encourage you to persevere in righteousness?

> Consider it a great joy, my brothers and sisters, whenever you experience various trials, because you know that the testing of your faith produces endurance. And let endurance have its full effect, so that you may be mature and complete, lacking nothing.
>
> **JAMES 1:2-4**

> Blessed is the one who endures trials, because when he has stood the test he will receive the crown of life that God has promised to those who love him.
>
> **JAMES 1:12**

DAY 5

WHEREVER YOU GO

Ruth would prove to be worth more to Naomi than either of them could imagine.

When I moved to Nashville more than twenty years ago, I didn't know a single person. I knew of friends of friends, and a few people had scribbled on napkins names of acquaintances to look up since no one could text contacts back and forth. (It was basically the 1800s.) Before moving, I'd been in the same church, in the same city, with many of the same friends my entire life. My first few years in Nashville were terribly lonely, but eventually, I met my friend April, and then a few years later I met Paige and Mary Katharine, and now I have a church community I couldn't imagine life without. Having even one good friend in life gives you many things, not the least of which is the gift of not being alone. Naomi and Ruth had each other, and even though Naomi may have wanted to arrive in Bethlehem alone, Ruth would prove to be worth more to her than either of them could imagine.

READ RUTH 1:16-17.

> **PERSONAL TAKE:** Up to this point, Naomi had done almost all of the talking, but now it was Ruth's turn. Which of her statements resonates with you most and why?

Naomi's spewing bitterness, her discouraging pleas—Ruth had had enough. Despite Ruth's tearful grief, she silenced Naomi's complaints with her resolve.

> How did Ruth's loving yet firm words to Naomi affect the rest of their journey (v. 18)? Circle your answer.

Naomi . . .

got mad and ran ahead   disowned Ruth

stopped trying to persuade Ruth   wept

Ruth's resolute speech to Naomi emphasizes the power of the spoken word. She found her place in a long line of God's people who spoke truth at opportune moments. I think of Abigail speaking wisdom to David (1 Sam. 25:23-31), Jethro giving advice to Moses that helped him serve the people (Ex. 18:17-27), or Peter commanding a paralyzed man to "get up and walk!" (Acts 3:6). We could long recount the exchanges of Holy Spirit-filled men and women speaking life to the hopeless, despairing, deceived, rebellious, wounded. Ruth's words in 1:16-17 are not the stuff of knee-jerk responses. We can only reckon they were forged over time and in relationship with God. You don't decide to forsake all your gods and cling to a despairing in-law in a moment of whimsy. Ruth's words quieted Naomi (v. 18) because they'd been formed in love and loyalty.

Briefly sum up the central thought of each passage.

Proverbs 15:1-2,4

Proverbs 16:23-24

Proverbs 18:13

Proverbs 25:11

Proverbs 27:5-6

PERSONAL TAKE: How do these principles from Proverbs play out in Ruth's conversation with Naomi?

When I was a child, my dad was relentless at making us kids talk things out. We had more family meetings than I now have business meetings. I didn't love learning how to apologize or listen to others explain their point of view—couldn't we all just agree that my perspective was probably the right one? I'm indebted to my parents for teaching me how to have difficult conversations. Humble, truthful, and kind speech is healing ointment in bitter and complicated situations.

Since Ruth's words hold such weight, let's look at her speech more closely. Read the printed verses below.

· (Circle) the words that show Ruth's determination and strength.
· Underline the words that show her love and support for Naomi.
· ✓ Check the words that show her spiritual conviction.
· ✱ Star the words that show her humility.

(Mark words as many times as you think they apply.)

> But Ruth replied: Don't plead with me to abandon you or to return and not follow you. For wherever you go, I will go, and wherever you live, I will live; your people will be my people, and your God will be my God. Where you die, I will die, and there I will be buried. May the LORD punish me, and do so severely, if anything but death separates you and me.
> **RUTH 1:16-17**

NOW READ VERSE 18 AND TAKE IN NAOMI'S RESPONSE TO RUTH'S WORDS.

The CSB translation begins with "When Naomi saw . . ." It took Ruth's strong words to finally convince Naomi that she wasn't taking no for an answer. Our words have strength, especially when they're governed by the Holy Spirit. Sometimes we need to speak the hard word, the word of forgiveness, or the word of accepting forgiveness. Other times we need to speak the loving, determined, or committed word. Always the humble word.

Humble, truthful, and kind speech is healing ointment in bitter and complicated situations.

PERSONAL RESPONSE: Do you need to speak a word to someone? Matthew 5:23-24 talks about the importance of not delaying in certain circumstances. If you are sensing the Holy Spirit's nudge, write it here.

The verses we've studied today have been read at many weddings and printed on as many cards, gracing relationships since the day Ruth spoke them. But the truth is that this famous speech was uttered amidst loss and hardship and in the face of much bitterness. Ruth's words did not usher in a honeymoon but rather a permanent home in a foreign land.

As we consider this passage in light of New Testament realities, the questions become: *Are we committed to Christ? Will we go where He goes? Stay where He stays? Will His people be our people? His Father our Father?* I'm really looking forward to answering these questions with you over the next five sessions. You've already done a remarkable job.

WATCH

WATCH the Session Two video teaching and take notes below.

To access the video teaching sessions, use the instructions in the back of your Bible study book.

GRILLED SALMON WITH LEMON SAUCE

Salmon is pretty great no matter what, but what puts it over the top is how you dress it up. I love this recipe because you can still feel healthy while not skimping on what we all love—a good sauce. Add a green vegetable and you will feel even better about this meal. (SERVES 6)

INGREDIENTS FOR SALMON FILETS

2 garlic cloves, minced
2 tablespoons of olive oil
2 tablespoons of lemon juice
Salt and pepper to taste
6 salmon fillets

INGREDIENTS FOR SAUCE

2 tablespoons of butter
1 tablespoon of flour
⅔ cup of heavy cream
1 tablespoon of dijon mustard
½ teaspoon of paprika
2 tablespoons of water
Zest of 1 lemon
1 teaspoon of chopped basil

DIRECTIONS

1. In a small saucepan, melt butter, stir in flour, and cook until starting to brown. Whisk in salt and pepper to taste, paprika, cream, mustard, and water. Cook until simmering. Add basil and lemon zest. Set aside until ready to pour over salmon.

2. Heat the grill to 450°. In a small bowl, combine garlic, salt, pepper, oil, and lemon juice. Brush mixture over salmon. Grill turning once (6 minutes total).

3. Pour sauce over salmon and serve with sautéed spinach or your favorite green vegetable.

Turn to pages 184–187 for appetizer, side, and dessert ideas that go well with this dish.

ARRIVING

At the start of our summer vacations when I was little, my mom and dad would wake the four of us kids around two in the morning, carry us outside, and set us in the back of our light blue station wagon. They determined early on that driving on lack of sleep was better than driving while we kids were awake and doing all manner of annoying things. Because I am a product of the '80s, our summer excursions were without personal devices. It's nearly unfathomable what we endured. Eighteen hours of travel-Yahtzee® and Connect 4® with my siblings on I-95 South prepared me for many future trials.

Minter vacations remain in a class all their own. I don't know what your family vacations were like, but don't even try to argue this point with me. Most of this had to do with being on a pastor's budget. I don't regret this because the pastor's budget was precisely what inspired such creative corner-cutting. We stayed at a lot of free and inexpensive places that people from the church either recommended or allowed us to use. Occasionally the destinations were real disasters, but mostly we ended up with some special memories. The vehicles we took to get there posed the greatest challenges.

Whether it was the station wagon, four-cylinder, stick shift minivan, or my grandparents' sedan we borrowed just so we wouldn't break down, we broke down. Every time. Especially the minivan. It couldn't handle the six of us plus the cartop carrier, and it had a special malady called vapor lock that flared up on long trips. I know you've never heard of vapor lock before because you grew up in a normal family that went on normal vacations and took normal cars to get there, or you were a billionaire and you flew. We broke down so many times that my brother David grew up believing cars weren't designed to travel those kinds of distances. Like using a bicycle to get across the Atlantic, they just weren't made for that kind of thing.

For Naomi, her arrival marked a significant return to her homeland.

One of our favorite vacation spots was in New Hampshire, overlooking Lake Sunapee. It came with sailboats, a dinghy, kayaks, and a red and white Donzi® that belonged to the neighbor. He'd pull us around on tubes, kneeboards, and skis in water that never got above chilling even in July. When you're a kid you hardly notice these trifle details. Raspberry bushes lined the lake, trails snaked up verdant hills, and fishing occupied me for hours from the sloping wood dock that jutted out over clear waters. When I got up early enough, I'd cast alongside real fishermen, natives of the North and sea. A fisherman once asked me, "Fishin'-fuh-dinnah?" I kindly asked him six times to repeat himself before explaining, "No, I'm twelve, and my mom's making spaghetti tonight."

Then there was the cabin in Canada, owned by a wonderful but far more adventurous family in our church than the Minter clan could ever hope to be. Before we left, they stoked our anticipation with stories of piles of fresh blueberries and the lake with its turquoise hue. They forgot to mention the outhouse and the hatchet for chopping wood. It was a really amazing place for people who enjoy things like the wilderness. My dad could have stayed there a month, but my mom strangely doesn't do hatchets. And she contended you needed a machete just to get to the outhouse, assuming you were willing to go there in the first place.

The significantly bigger problem was the mouse that scurried across the floor, which is how my youngest sister described it when she cracked open the front door. My mom quickly clarified: it wasn't a mouse, and it didn't run. It was a rat that sauntered across the kitchen like it was the landlord. This particular rodent became the deal-breaker for everyone but Dad. But even he knew he couldn't expect his family to bunk with animals and borrow hatchets, no matter how cozy the crackling fires or fresh the blueberries. We found another cabin the next morning on Spectacle Lake with an indoor bathroom. Arriving never felt better.

If long and highly anticipated journeys make for extra spectacular arrivals, this week's study will not disappoint. We will witness Naomi pass through city gates she'd fled at least a decade prior, this time without her husband and children. Old friends and acquaintances enthusiastically greeted her, as old friends do. For Naomi, her arrival marked a significant return to her homeland. For Ruth, Bethlehem proved a foreign land, rife with challenges for a widowed Moabitess. But both arrived—and in a story that's already marked with bitter loss, weeping, and the tearing apart of two sisters-in-law, just this is reason for rejoicing.

THEY ARRIVED IN BETHLEHEM AT THE BEGINNING OF THE BARLEY HARVEST.

Ruth 1:22

DAY 1
COMING HOME

Israel wasn't only Naomi's home but the place of God's dwelling.

My friend took four of her young godchildren to her house to watch the scariest movie, hands-down, ever made: *The Wizard of Oz*. I told her this was a huge mistake. Kids under eight shouldn't be subjected to this movie because I was twenty the last time it scared me. I don't care how far cinematic technology has come; nothing is more terrifying than the green witch pedaling her bicycle through the air calling Dorothy "my pretty."[1]

Second to the witch are the monkeys, followed closely by the diminishing hourglass and a wizard who's the only one who can help but who ends up not really being a helpful wizard. Dorothy's only friends in Oz are a shrinking lion, a scarecrow who's missing a heart, and a tin man who has to oil himself to walk. But the true horror of this film is that Dorothy can't get home. Every other scary detail is merely a supporting cast member. It's why decades later we can all recite the movie's most memorable phrase, "There's no place like home. There's no place like home. There's no place like home."[2]

I'm assuming Naomi carried a similar sentiment on the long trek to Bethlehem. Truly life had taken multiple tragic turns since her departure. Interestingly, such tragedies would make Naomi's return either especially sweet, deeply bitter, or both. We will soon find out. I do wonder what Naomi was thinking as her tired steps hit the dust with ebbing hope that things might be different in Bethlehem. After all, Israel wasn't only Naomi's home but the place of God's dwelling.

CAREFULLY READ RUTH 1:19-21 TWO TIMES THROUGH.

On Naomi's return, "the whole town was excited" (v. 19). The Hebrew word translated "excited" or "stirred" is *wattēhōm*, which means "echoed with excitement." The word "conjures up images of joyous shouting and happy, animated conversations in response to an event. . . . Here one imagines excited citizens scurrying about the streets shouting the good news to others, who then do likewise."[3] Verse 19 also says the town was excited because of *their* arrival. This relays that not only Naomi's arrival caused a reaction.

PERSONAL TAKE: Given what we know about Moab's relationship with Israel, describe the significance of Naomi returning to Bethlehem with Ruth.

This stirring reception seems to indicate Naomi was not an obscure individual in Bethlehem but had been a well-loved, prominent person in her society. So much that her return set the entire town in a frenzy, the women exclaiming to one another, "Can this be Naomi?" (v. 19). This celebrated recognition didn't soothe Naomi's pain but seemed to exacerbate it. Naomi now stood empty-handed, a poignant contrast to the fullness by which she had once been known: married to a prominent man in Bethlehem, the mother of two sons, bearing the name Naomi, which literally means "pleasantness, delight," and being part of the chosen nation of Israel.[4] In her time and culture these collective attributes deemed her rich beyond measure. Contrast this imagery with the woman now standing at the gates of the city bereft of everything she held dear. Her only "belonging"? A foreign woman from a despised land.

Tim Keller helps us further understand the cultural ramifications of Naomi's desperate situation:

> It is difficult for us today to appreciate the significance of child-bearing in ancient times. We live in an individualistic age in which we tend to dream of individual success, achievement, and prominence. That was not true in ancient times. All aspirations and dreams were for your *family's* success and prominence. The family was your primary identity, not your vocation, friendships and so on. It was the bearer of all hopes and dreams. Therefore there was nothing more important than to have and raise children who loved and honored you and who walked in your ways. In light of this, female "barrenness" was considered the worse possible curse. A woman in this situation could not avoid feeling like a terrible failure.[6]

Keller writes here of women in ancient times who could not bear children, but this surely applies to Naomi who bore two sons but lost them.

> There was nothing more important than to have and raise children who loved and honored you and who walked in your ways.[5]
>
> **TIM KELLER**

PERSONAL TAKE: Every culture exalts certain primary sources of identity. What are some things our culture values as being essential for a worthy identity?

Keller's quote further helps us understand why Naomi told the women not to call her by her name anymore (v. 20).

Instead, she told them to call her _____, which means (circle your answer):

Bitter   Angry   Unforgiving   Depressed

Naomi made four statements that explain her request for a new name (vv. 20-21). Fill in the blanks below:

1. The _____ has made me very bitter.

2. I went away full, but the _____ has brought me back empty.

3. Why do you call me Naomi, since the _____ has opposed me?

4. The _____ has afflicted me.

PERSONAL TAKE: Why do you think Naomi blamed God for her suffering?

PERSONAL REFLECTION: What causes you to turn to God in suffering? On the other hand, what causes you to blame Him for it?

I have a few close friends and loved ones with chronic health conditions. Long-term suffering is one of the greatest challenges to our faith, though it can also be a boon to it as we experience God's presence and grace in the midst of our pain. Suffering naturally causes us to think we've been forgotten by God, or possibly worse—that what we're going through is from His hand. Reconciling our suffering with a good God whose love endures forever is an enduring challenge of the human condition.

Naomi wrestled in similar ways with similar questions. She charged God not only with oversight of her pain but also responsibility for it: *the Almighty has done this to me!* I remember feeling this during my sophomore year of college. I can't recall the dilemma, but I remember being so frustrated by the idea that God was purposefully against me that I punched my steering wheel so hard the horn ejected from its socket and pulsed up and down, hanging by a large spring. This made me even madder! (No one has ever accused me of being soothing.) So I can appreciate that Naomi's highly charged accusations were not edited out of the text. They're hardly proper Sunday morning fare. Yet who cannot relate at some point during her life?

READ THE FOLLOWING VERSES. Next to each verse, describe the writer's suffering and how he saw God in it.

Job 9:16-19 (Job)

Psalm 22:1-2 (David)

Psalm 88:6-9 (sons of Korah)

Lamentations 3:7-9 (Jeremiah)

Matthew 27:45-46 (Jesus)

How often do we feel forsaken by God, angry or bitter, yet we don't stop to address our feelings with Him? We drown our inner cries and questions in a sea of entertainment. Some may pour an extra drink or burn off anxiety at the gym. Others may post on social media for the dopamine hits of likes and comments. What about staying longer at the office when perhaps what is in order is a good read through Jeremiah's book of Lamentations? Or a read through Mark's Gospel (Mark, who emphasizes the sufferings of Christ and His followers)? How much might we need solitude in the presence of Christ or times of prayer with friends instead of the ways we choose to numb ourselves?

> God wants the true state of our hearts more than our "right" answers.

Perhaps we're afraid of what we'll experience when we get in God's presence. Maybe we're fearful we won't hear anything from Him, that He'll require something of us we don't want to give, or that we'll learn something about ourselves we don't want to know. Perhaps it's too much work. Or maybe we fear erupting like Naomi or punching our steering wheels.

Regardless of your fears, I encourage you to sit before the Lord with the true state of your heart (anger, fear, grief, questions, doubt, numbness, unbelief . . .). He is God enough to handle whatever you bring to Him. In the book of Lamentations, Jeremiah brought his raw and honest thoughts and emotions to the Lord, but he landed on: *You're still faithful . . . You heard me . . . You came near.*

Lean into this closing prayer. While we all love a day of study where we fill in blanks and jot down correct answers, God wants the true state of our hearts more than our "right" answers—even if they're a little explosive like Naomi's.

> **PRAYER:** Read this portion of Jeremiah's prayer: Lamentations 3:21-33,55-58. Take some time to be honest with yourself and with God. Sit quietly before Him with your questions and the state of your heart. If you're in a peaceful place with Him, thank Him for this gift of peace and rest.

DAY 2
A HOPEFUL GLIMMER

When my sister Megan was ten, she penned her first novel, *Why Don't You Like Me, Aunt Bess?* Our family couldn't get past the opening line: "Jane went to live with her Aunt Bess because her parents were killed on the way to a potluck." Why tarry with needless and encumbering details when you can just get on with it? Megan's dilemma is that of any good writer who has a story to tell—how to give the reader context (why Jane was living with her aunt who apparently didn't like her) while not spending too much time on the details. Megan's solution was to accomplish this in one sentence. Our family loves this story.

Certainly, Ruth's author wasn't mindlessly rushing through the details of the first chapter; it is brilliantly told. I do, however, get the impression he was anxious to get to a story of redemption that he couldn't tell without first giving the essential backstory. What began with six characters—Elimelech, Naomi, Mahlon, Chilion, Ruth, and Orpah—has reduced to an unlikely pair, Naomi and Ruth. We can read the first chapter in a couple of minutes, potentially obscuring the weight of the famine, the move, the marriage of two sons, the death of a husband, the death of two sons, the beginning of a return journey, the turning back of one woman, and now the arrival in Bethlehem. Despite the narrator's economy of words, we should allow the gravity of these events to settle into our understanding. This was no easy decade.

As the narrator begins to close this chapter both literally and figuratively, he leaves us with the subtle hint that maybe—just maybe—our story is about to take a hopeful turn.

> As the narrator begins to close this chapter both literally and figuratively, he leaves us with the subtle hint that maybe—just maybe—our story is about to take a hopeful turn.

REREAD CHAPTER 1 OF RUTH WITHOUT INTERRUPTION.
What stands out to you after looking at it as a whole?

In verse 22, what new title did the narrator give Ruth?

Why do you think Scripture highlights Ruth's nationality at this point in the story?

Look back at verse 22. When did Naomi and Ruth arrive?

After hardship and suffering, we get a faint glimpse that perhaps God had not been absent after all. Could it be that He has long been working behind the scenes, under the soil, and now His goodness is cropping up above the ground as the barley harvest is beginning? Though it's still too early in the story to know what God is up to, I love this quote by biblical commentator Robert Hubbard, "When God is at work, bitter hopelessness can be the beginning of some surprising good."[7] This surprising good will prove even more significant given that Ruth is a Moabitess. Up until this point in the story, the narrator simply called her Ruth. He now adds "the Moabitess" to remind us how unlikely from a human perspective any success whatsoever will be for her in the land of Bethlehem.

> **PERSONAL RESPONSE:** What is something you've prayed or waited for over a long period of time? Have you seen a glimpse—no matter how small—that God is working? Are there any promises in Scripture you're clinging to? Write about it below.

The beginning of the barley harvest may not thrill your heart like it would have for ancient readers, but this was God's assurance of provision. Every grain of barley represents opportunity, sustenance, hope, and the reminder of God's presence and perfect timing—Ruth and Naomi's return coincided with God's coming to the aid of His people.

Because Ruth and Naomi's story up to this point hinges on verse 22 and because Scripture has much to say about harvests, we'll survey some verses outside the book of Ruth. Even though most of us don't live in agrarian societies, the idea of harvest season always applies. If you're in a season of harvesting, you need to start hauling it in. If you're not, it's a great time to start throwing out seed. It's always just a matter of what side of the harvest you're on, sowing or reaping. Both are good and necessary seasons of life.

PERSONAL REFLECTION: Before we read passages about harvests, are you in a season of sowing, reaping, or both? Explain why.

READ GENESIS 8:22. How long will seedtime and harvest endure?

READ EXODUS 34:21. True/False: According to Old Testament law, one should rest on the seventh day during the plowing season but not during harvest.

READ LEVITICUS 23:9-14. According to the law, what were the Israelites to do with the first grain of their harvest?

How can we apply the Exodus and Leviticus principles to our modern lives?

READ JEREMIAH 5:24. Jeremiah's complaint against the people he prophesied to was that they did not regard God in what way?

Most of us have to make contextual leaps to appreciate the significance of a rich harvest in due season. The closest I come are my raised garden beds that yield summer tomatoes, peppers, okra, herbs, and zinnias. I'm a committed fan of ordering my Thanksgiving turkey from a local farm, and occasionally I get to my local farmer's market. Beyond that, you will find me wandering the aisles of the grocery store. I seldom thought about farming until my mid-thirties when my local farm sent emails that included statements like: "No eggs this week because the chickens won't lay in this heat," "The price of honey is going up because bees are mysteriously disappearing," and "Would anyone like a sugar-cured pork jowl?" I feel like the answer is no, but what's a jowl?

Though I still don't get all that close to the process, I newly appreciate what it means to depend on God's grace to water the soil, bring the sun, and keep all the symbiotic relationships going while sustaining the farmers' health. It is a good reminder of God's creativity and precision. All good things come from His hand, whether we get our food straight from the ground or bagged from the supermarket.

Since we've looked at a few biblical references regarding the physical process of harvesting, I can't help but look at the process that affects most of us more immediately—the spiritual process of sowing and reaping. I want us to look at Psalm 126. Keep in mind it's written from the perspective of Israelite exiles returning home from Babylon (much like Naomi returning home from Moab). Here the psalmist spoke in metaphorical terms of the believer's pilgrimage and her harvest.[8]

> **READ PSALM 126.** What action often comes before reaping "with shouts of joy" (v. 5)?

> What do our weeping and our seed turn to (v. 6)?

> **PERSONAL RESPONSE:** Practically speaking, how can you sow in your weeping?

Every time I read this passage, I'm reminded that it is not our weeping that brings the harvest but our sowing. We can grieve and shed tears, but no harvest will come unless we simultaneously cast our seed. This is rarely easy. Difficult seasons don't normally motivate us to yell, "Put me in, Coach!" But as we learned in last session's study of Ruth and Orpah, what we do while we're weeping makes all the difference.

> Let us not get tired of doing good, for we will reap at the *proper time* if we do not give up.
> **GALATIANS 6:9** (*EMPHASIS MINE*)

Could you use a glimpse of God breaking through the long barren land of a certain season? Do not give up; keep sowing. God is faithful, and He has not forgotten you. He sees your labor of love and His promises to you will not fail (Heb. 6:10-12). At just the right time, the barley harvest will begin, and you may just so happen to be arriving.

DAY 3
A MYSTERIOUS RELATIVE

If this story were a movie, we'd be about thirty-five minutes in—right about the place where you start committing to the story line and characters. It's when you start asking yourself, *Am I hooked, or is the popcorn keeping me here?* It's where reality is suspended and you start identifying with certain characters, bracing yourself for the sudden appearance of the suspicious-looking person who is probably going to change, well, everything. If the new character is dashing and good and a smidge mysterious, it's when you commit to the full two hours. Enter Boaz.

Ruth's story is part of the much larger story of God's ongoing redemptive plan.

TODAY WE BEGIN A NEW CHAPTER. READ RUTH 2:1-3.

We'll take these verses one by one because each is important to the story. Get ready for a little Bible flipping and some slightly more technical information. It will help give more meaning when the curtain opens on chapter 2.

Verse 1. Ruth's story is part of the much larger story of God's ongoing redemptive plan. Since Boaz is a prominent character, it will help us to know where he comes from and how he's related to some other important characters.

From what clan (some Bible translations say "family") was Boaz? Circle your answer.

Perez   Judah   David   Elimelech

You'll remember from Session Two that Elimelech, Naomi, and their two sons came from Bethlehem-Judah, part of the nation of Israel. Israel was divided into twelve tribes, which began with the twelve sons of Jacob. One of the most significant is the tribe of Judah, which we will later discover includes Elimelech. Its importance becomes paramount as history unfolds, so hang onto this information.

Summarize what you've just read by filling in the following: Boaz was from the nation of _____, the tribe of _____, and the clan/family of _____.

A clan was a subgroup of a tribe consisting of several families. So verse 1 tells us that Naomi had a significant relative named Boaz from her husband's clan. From a modern, western perspective, this might make us think, *Oh good, Naomi's got a place to spend the holidays. We were worried!* But for an Israelite of the day, "this small detail raises the interest and hopes of the readers, especially those who are familiar with Israelite family law and custom."[9] The fact that Naomi had a living relative from her husband's side of the family was a sign of tremendous hope. But we'll expound upon this more in future days. For now, note that Boaz's relation to Naomi was significant to her beyond turkey dinners and *It's a Wonderful Life* reruns. He was from Elimelech's clan, the tribe of Judah, and the nation of Israel.

Now that we know about Boaz's lineage, describe what we're told about him as a person (vv. 1,3).

The original language in verse 1 gives us an even richer picture. The Hebrew term for "man of standing" is an *'iš gibbôr hayil*, which most often means "war hero," "capable person," "wealthy man."[10] This doesn't mean Boaz had a military background; rather, it's a term that means "high social standing." In short, he was a powerful person—someone whose wealth and high reputation in Bethlehem gave him strong influence among his peers.

Verse 2. Verse 2 shifts the focus back to Ruth asking Naomi if she can go to the fields to pick up leftover grain. This seems to have no relation to its preceding verse, but it will connect for us soon. Again, the narrator was using the title "Ruth the Moabitess," which we first saw in Ruth 1:22. Notice what the author seems to be doing: While Ruth resided in Moab, he referred to her as Ruth, but upon her arrival in Bethlehem, he twice called her "Ruth the Moabitess." The narrator went out of his way to further highlight how unlikely any success would be for Ruth, an outsider from a land totally hostile to Israel, as well as to Israel's God. "Moabitess" is the condemning tag that could forever be her downfall, the piece of information that gnaws at her heels, that ruins her chances of ever becoming someone in Israel. Hers was a tarnished heritage she was powerless to change.

PERSONAL TAKE: What are some things about your own history or your family's history that bother you in your quietest moments, that make you think God can never really love or use you? (Be as honest with your answer as you can).

God's tender heart for the outcast was expressed all the way back in Old Testament law. We think of such acceptance beginning with Christ, but really it was fulfilled in Him; God has always been concerned about the lowly, the poor, the outsider. If we didn't understand this about God's heart, we might think it odd for Ruth to have been given the liberty of gleaning from a field in Bethlehem-Judah.

READ LEVITICUS 19:9-10; 23:22 AND DEUTERONOMY 10:18-19; 24:19-22.

Describe the Old Testament law pertaining to landowners and how this law affected Ruth's right to glean.

What do these laws tell us about God's heart for the poor, foreigner, and widow?

> God's tender heart for the outcast was expressed all the way back in Old Testament law.

Although this law should have been well followed, Ruth had only hoped to find someone in whose eyes she could find favor. This may mean she was unfamiliar with Jewish law, or it may simply mean that because God's people don't always hold to His commands, she was hoping for someone who would actually honor God's law of allowing a foreigner to glean. It's possible many of the landowners were selfish or hostile to a widowed Moabitess gleaning on their land. Either way, Ruth was looking for someone gracious.

Verse 3. Next, we learn "Ruth left and entered the field to gather grain behind the harvesters." I'm not sure if gleaning apples is an actual thing or not, but it's the closest context I have. My parents used to take us kids apple picking every October. My dad was big on training us in integrity, so the apple orchard held a host of teaching moments. He would remind us to only eat the apples that were already on the ground, while all the ones we picked off the tree had to be put in the bag to later be weighed and paid for. I was not above shaking a tree to produce more ground-lying apples. That was the first thing I tried every year even though I don't even really like apples that much. To this day I think it was my dad's law producing sin in me (a Rom. 7:8 joke).

It's hard enough having to glean for ourselves, but I find Ruth's outstanding work ethic compelling. She was unwilling for time to pass before asserting herself for the benefit of her and Naomi's livelihood. I imagine Ruth was more motivated by wanting to provide for Naomi than even herself. We'll eventually come back to this important quality of hard work, but for now, I want to look at one of the most fascinating turn of events in this story.

Verse 3 says Ruth "happened" to find herself working in whose field?

PERSONAL TAKE: How does Ruth "happening" upon Boaz's field strike you? Luck, coincidence, providence? Explain your thoughts.

Yahweh:
the Hebrew name for the God of the covenant

Surprisingly, this Hebrew phrase means "Ruth's chance chanced" upon Boaz's field. It's a purposefully redundant phrase that means "a stroke of luck."[11] The writer is employing a literary technique that elicits awareness from the reader that Ruth stumbling upon the field of Boaz is more than just casual coincidence. We're supposed to sit up and say, "Wait just a minute here—this can't be luck!" We're prompted to start looking for the invisible hand of Yahweh.

Though God's hand of providence is at work here, how did Ruth's work ethic set her up for such a divine blessing?

PERSONAL RESPONSE: Can you think of a time when you were faithfully going about a routine task or job and you "happened" upon someone or something special? If you have one, journal below and plan to share the experience with your small group.

Even though we've only looked at three verses today, we've covered a lot of ground. My hope is that we've gleaned a heightened sense of what God is doing all around us, even in the seemingly mundane, and that we remember how purposeful He is, how intently He carves our paths, authors each stroke, and directs our courses into others' lives.

As Elizabeth Barrett Browning put it,

> Earth's crammed with heaven,
> And every common bush afire with God:
> But only he who sees, takes off his shoes,
> The rest sit round it, and pluck blackberries,
> And daub their natural faces unaware.[12]

I don't want to miss the divine for the blackberries. Oh Lord, give us eyes to see!

DAY 4
ALL IN A DAY'S WORK

The poetry of the Bible is beautiful and powerful. It has been written with imagination, and it needs to be read with imagination.[14]

DR. KNUT HEIM

One of my favorite seminary professors, Dr. Knut Heim, writes, "The poetry of the Bible is beautiful and powerful. It has been written with imagination, and it needs to be read with imagination."[13] Though Ruth is a historical book, not a poetry book, his words apply. We receive the most from Scripture when we slip into the shoes of the characters we read about, ask questions of the text, take note of the atmosphere. Imaginative reading is not fanciful reading. It is not extracting from the text what isn't there, nor is it tailoring the text to our desires or cultural norms. But imaginative reading does engage our senses, emotions, wonderings, and intellect.

In addition to engaging my imagination, I'll share a few of my Bible reading practices that may be helpful as we study the book of Ruth.

First, I almost always see something special in the Scriptures when I come to God hungry. Approaching the Word desirous to be filled is important. When I don't have that longing, I tell the Lord. He can speak to us in whatever state we're in, but asking the Holy Spirit to show us wonderful things out of His Word is of great benefit (Ps. 119:18).

Second, I keep an eye out for objects, people, phrases, descriptions—whatever might make me think more intently about what's happening in my reading. I ask questions! I notice my own emotions. Does the passage excite me, convict me, warm me, make me mad? This may reveal where my heart is soft and where it's resistant to the ways of Christ.

Third, I try to bridge what I'm reading to my life and the lives around me. This doesn't mean I pull passages out of context or make the Bible "all about me." Rather, after having considered things like cultural context, the original intent of the author, and the theological framework, I'm eager to make connections and applications to my personal life. Some applications will be more practical than others, but all are important.

Let's start by practicing some of these approaches. First, let's ask the Holy Spirit to open our eyes to see what we could never see on our own.

READ RUTH 2:4-7. Write any phrases, words, or descriptions that are meaningful to you. Also, note any questions you have.

In verse 4, "Just then Boaz arrived from Bethlehem" (NIV) stands out to me. Some translations say, "Now behold" or "Later, when." "Just then" gives us the sense that God was orchestrating Ruth and Boaz's meeting. After reading that Ruth returned to Bethlehem just as the barley harvest was beginning and that she happened to find herself working in Boaz's field, it's hard to miss that *just then* Boaz arrived exactly where Ruth was working. We touched on God's providence yesterday, but here is another instance of His hidden hand arranging Boaz and Ruth's first encounter.

PERSONAL REFLECTION: In what area of your life are you struggling with God's timing? How does this reminder of His providence over time, places, and encounters encourage you to trust His perfect timing in your own life?

According to verse 4, how did Boaz greet his workers, and how did they reply?

PERSONAL TAKE: What does this simple exchange tell us about Boaz and the work environment he fostered?

When Boaz noticed Ruth, he was intrigued. He asked the manager of his workers whose young woman she was. This is a good spot for imaginative reading. We should be asking ourselves questions like, *What about Ruth caught Boaz's eye? Why didn't he address her directly? Why was it important to whom Ruth belonged?* We may not always get answers to our questions, but we should be inquiring as we go.

Where we come from and what kind of blood runs through our veins is not nearly as impactful as our character and reputation.

According to verses 6-7, what did the foreman say about each category below?

Ruth's heritage:

Ruth's work ethic:

It's possible Boaz asked the foreman about Ruth because it was culturally inappropriate to address a woman directly.[15] And he may have asked to whom she belonged because she was out of place among his workers in his fields. Boaz asked a simple question, but the servant offered additional detail. *She's a Moabitess who came back with Naomi, but what's really impressive is how incredibly hard-working she is—how she's gleaned nonstop from morning till now, except for this one tiny rest in the shelter!* Perhaps the servant reminds us that where we come from and what kind of blood runs through our veins is not nearly as impactful as our character and reputation.

Proverbs 22:1 seems a fitting caption for the scene. What is more desirable than riches and more esteemed than silver or gold? Circle your answer.

An impressive pedigree   How many children you have

A good name   A humble spirit

Ruth was making a name for herself through her commitment to Naomi and her determination in the fields. She wasn't afraid to do the hard work and take her place in a foreign and somewhat hostile environment. How easy it can be in our western culture of excess and immediacy to minimize the value of a strong work ethic. Certainly, many among us work tirelessly for ourselves and our loved ones. Yet Ruth's pluck and fortitude is a healthy reminder for me, in the age of binge-watching, social media scrolling, and buy-now-pay-later, that God delights in a faithful worker.

PERSONAL RESPONSE: Look back at verses 6-7. What impresses you most about Ruth's work ethic?

Read the following verses about work and answer the corresponding questions.

READ GENESIS 2:15-22. God gave Adam (and later Eve) work to do in a perfect environment before sin and brokenness entered the world. What does this say about the nature of work?

READ ECCLESIASTES 9:10. How does the author encourage us to work?

READ PROVERBS 14:23. What does the author say about the difference between "hard work" and "endless talk"?

READ PROVERBS 6:6-11. What creature should inspire us toward hard work and why?

READ COLOSSIANS 3:22-24. How did the apostle Paul encourage those enslaved in Colossae to view their work?

We can take much away from Ruth's outstanding work ethic. She saw no task as beneath her. She didn't let fear of the unknown or a foreign territory stop her. She sought out her work and didn't wait for it to come to her (v. 7).

Though our work bears the heaviness of sin's curse on creation (Gen. 3:17-19), it is still a gift. Work not only brings blessing; it is the blessing.

PERSONAL RESPONSE: How has today's study helped you think differently about your work?

God's providence was all over Ruth's encounters, yet it was her obedience and work that placed her in the way of His providence. It's a mystery I don't fully understand, but I believe that working as unto the Lord positions us in God's pathways.

It's not what we accomplish for God but what we do with Him that matters.

PERSONAL REFLECTION: How has God used your work, no matter how impressive or humble, to show you His presence and activity in your life?

Some of us work too much and need to be intentional about rest and time with family and friends. Others are on the opposite end, too often sitting idle while waiting for the perfect job to drop in our laps. The story of God's providence intersecting with Ruth's work in the fields is a glorious mystery. And whether or not Ruth understood the biblical concept that all work is sacred when done unto God, she seemed to understand that even the menial tasks mattered. I don't have to go back more than a decade or so to remember the many humbling jobs I did while pursuing a singing and then writing career. The paint brushes and paint cans, the mowers and dumpsters remind me God delights in pure hearts and dedicated hands. It's not what we accomplish for Him but what we do with Him that matters.

DAY 5

A FIRST ENCOUNTER

Today's bend in Ruth's story will not be nearly as hard on us as yesterday's. We can wipe the sweat from our brows and settle in for a much-anticipated conversation between Ruth and Boaz. How delightful to cap off our week with a budding romance, friendship, or random meeting—we're not sure which one yet.

> Now to him who is able to do above and beyond all that we ask or think according to the power that works in us.
>
> **EPHESIANS 3:20**

THOUGHTFULLY READ RUTH 2:8-9. Take in Boaz's very first words to Ruth and list the specific instructions he gave her.

Ruth hoped to pick up grain behind anyone showing her favor (see v. 2). How did Boaz's kindness exceed her highest hopes?

Ruth's unexpected blessings from Boaz remind me of Ephesians 3:20, which says that God is able to do more than all we can ask or imagine.

PERSONAL REFLECTION: What's something God has done in your life that far exceeded what you could have asked for or dreamed of? Jot it down for discussion later.

In verse 9, Boaz told Ruth that whenever she was thirsty, she could drink from the jars the young men filled. This seems to be a simple act of kindness, but according to ancient customs, Boaz made an extraordinary offer. We'll need to flip back in the Old Testament and forward to John's Gospel to see why this is so significant.

What two types of people drew water?

"A foreign woman who customarily would draw water *for* Israelites was welcome to drink water drawn *by* Israelites."[16] What an unexpected offer in a day when women and servants were typically the ones drawing and serving water. Customarily speaking, this was a profound offer because it elevated Ruth's status. It was also a logistical blessing. Water was more than likely drawn outside the gates of Bethlehem and then had to be carried in jars to the fields. The time and energy involved were significant, making Boaz's offer for Ruth to freely drink even more valuable.

> **PERSONAL RESPONSE:** Briefly write about a time when someone treated you with excessive kindness or generosity. What did this tell you about the character of God?

Not only did Boaz provide for Ruth, but he took a stand to protect her. In a world where power was often abused for selfish and oppressive ends, Boaz wielded his strength and stature on behalf of the vulnerable. Verse 9 says Boaz ordered his men "not to touch" Ruth. This expression means, "to strike, harass, take advantage of, or mistreat."[17] One commentator smartly states, "Boaz is hereby instituting the first anti-sexual-harassment policy in the workplace recorded in the Bible."[18] He is showing *ḥesed* to Ruth—the widow, the foreigner, the lowly, the poor.

> Write the definition of *ḥesed*. (See p. 24 for a reminder.)

The book of Ruth is continually driving toward the message of Christ and the gospel, and the beginning of this exchange between Boaz and Ruth reminds us of this. We see in Boaz a reminder of Jesus's heart for the vulnerable and overlooked.

ONCE AGAIN, HOLD YOUR PLACE IN RUTH AND READ JOHN 4:1-42.
This is a longer than normal passage, but I don't want you to miss any part of such a redemptive story. As you read, look for parallels to what we're studying in Ruth.

What did both Boaz and Jesus offer Ruth and the Samaritan woman, respectively?

What does John 4:9 reveal about the relationship between Jews and Samaritans? How is this similar to Ruth and Boaz's relationship?

Ruth was a widow. The woman at the well was also in a place of vulnerability. Describe her situation according to verses 17-18.

How did the disciples respond when they came upon Jesus speaking with this woman?

PERSONAL TAKE: Do you see any other parallels or similarities to what you've studied in the book of Ruth?

A several-times-over divorced woman from Samaria would have been lowly regarded by Jewish men. Certainly, the disciples assumed Jesus was much too important, much too on a mission to be slowed down by the trivial needs of a Samaritan woman. Much more, what impression might this interaction give to pious Jews? Yet Jesus reordered the priorities of His disciples. Entrance to His kingdom is not about how connected, religiously put together, or powerful a person is. On the contrary, the kingdom of heaven belongs to those who receive Jesus as Messiah, who understand their need for Him. Intentionally approaching this woman and revealing His nature to her is the unexpected way of Christ. He offers Himself and His reign to those who joyfully receive Him, knowing they have nothing to give in return.

> **PERSONAL REFLECTION:** So far, how is the book of Ruth giving you a picture of the lavish news of the gospel? Think of themes of generosity, unexpected kindness, grace, and counter-cultural gestures.

In the best of scenarios, Ruth would have been ignored and unnoticed—in the worst of them, harassed and abused. Boaz broke through the cultural norms with the *ḥeseḏ* of God by esteeming and protecting her. This takes nothing away from the strength and fortitude of Ruth. Her place in the gospel story is extraordinary. But the reality of her position in a male-dominated Israelite society built on marriage and hostility to the people of Moab left her as vulnerable as the Samaritan woman at the well. It is precisely into this scenario Boaz shone forth with the love of God. Scholar Daniel I. Block puts it like this, "From the first time Boaz opens his mouth until the last words he utters (4:9-10), his tone exudes compassion, grace, and generosity. In the man who speaks to this Moabite field worker biblical *ḥeseḏ* becomes flesh and dwells among humankind."[19]

PERSONAL RESPONSE: How do you see God's ultimate _hesed_ becoming flesh and dwelling among us in John 4?

Grace:

undeserved acceptance and love received from another, especially the characteristic attitude of God in providing salvation for sinners

Perhaps after reading the accounts in Ruth and John you're still thinking, *My history is too blemished. I'm not worth that kind of care.* Remember that both Ruth and the Samaritan woman were unlikely candidates for the generosity they received given the cultural norms in which they found themselves. The care Boaz showed Ruth was but a glimpse of the redemption Jesus provided for the woman at the well—grace where it could never be earned. It's the redemption He shows each of us no matter our pasts.

REFLECT ON ROMANS 5:6-8 BELOW.

While we were still helpless, at the right time, Christ died for the ungodly. For rarely will someone die for a just person— though for a good person perhaps someone might even dare to die. But God proves his own love for us in that while we were still sinners, Christ died for us.

May the gospel's truth silence every accusing voice and wipe out every guilty thought. The kingdom of heaven is for you if you will simply receive it. In the book of Ruth and John's Gospel, we see God's heart is bent toward the vulnerable. We have only begun to draw from the deep well of His kindness.

WATCH

WATCH the Session Three video teaching and take notes below.

To access the video teaching sessions, use the instructions in the back of your Bible study book.

LEMON GREEK CHICKEN SOUP

I love soup. I will serve it regardless of the season. I've been known to make it in July and August without apology. This is a Regina Pinto specialty, one of my dear friends and coauthor of our cookbook A Place at the Table. *This is the perfect blend of healthy and tasty. Serve with bread and have some friends over—they will love you for it.* (SERVES 6)

INGREDIENTS

12 cups of chicken broth

3 tablespoons of olive oil

Zest of 1 lemon

1 medium onion, chopped

3 garlic cloves

2 celery sticks

3 peeled carrots

1 tablespoon of salt

3 boneless chicken breasts

1 cup couscous or long grain rice

Freshly chopped parsley

½ cup of lemon juice

Salt and pepper to taste

DIRECTIONS

1. Place olive oil, onion, and garlic on medium-low heat. Sauté for 3–4 minutes to soften. Add chicken broth, chicken breast, vegetables, and salt and pepper to taste. Cover and boil on high heat. When starting to boil, reduce heat to medium and let it simmer for 1 hour.

2. Remove chicken breasts and set them aside. Strain the stock and then put it back in the pot. Shred the chicken.

3. Put the pot back on high heat and add the couscous or rice. Let it boil until the couscous or rice is cooked; then add back the shredded chicken. Add lemon juice to taste.

4. Serve sprinkled with parsley and some crumbled feta cheese and lemon zest. Add salt and pepper as needed.

 Turn to pages 184–187 for appetizer, side, and dessert ideas that go well with this dish.

AN ENCOUNTER

When Mary Katharine, my friend and Executive Director of JMI, called one day to see if I wanted to take a private plane to an obscure city in the jungle to meet with indigenous jungle pastors, my response was concise: "Absolutely. I'll tell my mom after we're back." (Even as a full-fledged adult there are still things you wait to tell your mom.) After having traveled for more than a decade to Manaus, the capital city of the state of Amazonas in Brazil, branching out deeper into the jungle was a golden opportunity. I realize that not everyone would view this as "golden," and some might even think "opportunity" a stretch, but for me, it had been on my list of things I'd been wanting to do.

Despite being a relatively cautious person by nature and not a huge risk-taker, I can be talked into certain oddball adventures with mystifying ease. It's a dichotomy. I have yet to determine why I can get really hung up over the possibility of getting someone's sore throat, but I have no issue getting on a prop plane and flying across the vast jungles of the Amazon. I will leave this to the therapists.

In Manaus, we boarded the eight-seater that was headed to the jungle city of Tefé. For the next ninety minutes, we passed over more trees than I'd seen in my lifetime—it was like flying over an endless crown of broccoli. My senses were overwhelmed sheerly from the jungle's pure vastness. Then there was the moment my friend Kari decided to read the placard she'd pulled from the side compartment. (Note to the wise: don't look for fine print of any sort while flying above a primordial void that would swallow you whole if you went down.) The now off-limits placard read, very casually mind you, "This is an experimental aircraft." That was fun to read in the air. And on the outbound flight, no less. Unless we felt better canoeing home, this experimental plane was also our ride back.

Living fully for Christ—and all the people and serving and joy and hardship that entails—is what matters in this life.

69

By all accounts, the experiment went well, praise be to the Lord, and we landed in Tefé. A Brazilian pastor greeted us and showed us to his pickup truck that seated five in the cab and two in the truck's bed. The pilots volunteered for the bed and jostled around quite a bit back there. I was concerned for their safety; the only thing worse than flying on an experimental aircraft is not having pilots to fly it back. We winded through hundreds of motorcyclists and paid no attention to road signs, serenaded by honking horns. I took in the foreign surroundings, pondering my arrival in such an out-of-the-way place.

We were there to meet a handful of indigenous jungle pastors who were serving their region of the Solimoes River. Paolo, Maria, Pedro, Jonas—they are the Boazs, the Ruths, the Naomis of the modern world (though not necessarily in modern settings). Like Ruth, they cashed in their worldly attachments for a life fully committed to God and His people. In the spirit of Boaz, they use whatever resources they have to extend love and tangible support to the surrounding villages. Children with myriad challenges, the ailing elderly, the hungry—it's an endless river of physical and spiritual needs. Some, like Naomi, have weathered profound losses yet are still hanging on to God's faithfulness to bring about a harvest in His time.

To be in their midst was a coveted privilege, a reminder that Ruths, Boazs, and Naomis are alive today, changing history, bending legacies in new directions, and storing up an eternal weight of glory (2 Cor. 4:17). They inspired me yet again that living fully for Christ—and all the people and serving and joy and hardship that entails—is what matters in this life. All else will dry and wither. Sitting in their presence was worth the experimental aircraft and even the dreaded possibility of catching a sore throat.

MAY YOU RECEIVE A
FULL REWARD FROM
THE LORD GOD OF ISRAEL,
UNDER WHOSE WINGS YOU
HAVE COME FOR REFUGE.

Ruth 2:12

DAY 1
UNEXPECTED KINDNESS

I want us to marvel at God's design of man and woman and the ways we need each other.

Last week we closed in the middle of a conversation between Ruth and Boaz. We can either attribute this to extremely poor planning on my part or consider it an effective literary technique that left you on the edge of your seat. We concluded with Boaz's first words to Ruth: an offer to stay working in his field, protection from potentially abusive male workers, and the gift of freely drinking the water the servants had drawn. Boaz exemplifies the power of kindness.

In the twelve years since the first iteration of this study, the cultural landscape of what is acceptable and tolerable in encounters between men and women has shifted significantly. In our cultural moment in the West, we're less likely to look for strong, wealthy males swooping in to save damsels in distress. We're more likely to expect independent, self-made women who can take care of themselves, who don't particularly need men. Because cultures ebb and flow on what they value in men and women, I appeal to you to witness Boaz's kindness to Ruth and Ruth's remarkable strength without looking through notably patriarchal or feminist lenses. We may be tempted to force both characters into a mold influenced by our own culture and experiences, but my hope is that we can at least momentarily step away from our gender biases and perceptions and simply delight in the goodness and strength found in each individual. I want us to marvel at God's design of man and woman and the ways we need each other. To let God speak into our cultural moment.

READ RUTH 2:8-11. For continuity, I'm including the passage we left off with last week.

Why was Ruth so surprised by Boaz's favor (v. 10)?

True/False: Boaz noticed Ruth because of her exquisite beauty.

In verse 11, Boaz detailed what impressed him about Ruth. List the specifics in your own words.

PERSONAL REFLECTION: What is meaningful to you about Boaz recognizing Ruth for what she did and the type of woman she was instead of solely for her physical attributes?

PERSONAL TAKE: How could you be more intentional about noticing the hearts of one another over and above beauty and status?

Boaz was impressed with Ruth for reasons that went beyond beauty, heritage, culture, status, and wealth.

Physical beauty and attractiveness can rightly be appreciated. I have so many friends, both men and women, whose features I think are just stunning. But our culture puts entirely too much emphasis on physical appearance. It takes intentionality to encourage the attributes that flow from a person's heart. For instance, my friend April will serve your socks off; my sister-in-law Megen is exceptionally present for her children; my pastor leads with humility; my neighbor is walking through a significant trial with remarkable faith and courage. These are the kinds of things I want to celebrate in others. I will still get excited about your wavy hair, big brown eyes, and cool new shoes, but your character is what I want to treasure above all.

Boaz was impressed with Ruth for reasons that went beyond beauty, heritage, culture, status, and wealth. Even if she stood out for her physical beauty, Ruth was a foreign woman from the enemy land of Moab with no husband, children, resources, or elite status. Remarkably, one of the most powerful men in Bethlehem noticed her for something that transcends possessions, race, or physical appearance—her character. Ruth's story circulated to the top, not because of her agent or publicist, but because of the *ḥesed* she had shown her mother-in-law, the loss of her husband, the courage to leave her homeland and family, and the bravery to plant roots with a people she didn't know.

PERSONAL TAKE: Do you think Ruth thought she'd ever be noticed for her acts of service to Naomi or the sacrifices she made in leaving Moab? Why or why not?

The Lord loves to honor quiet and humble sacrifices, bringing them to light in His perfect time. Much like Ruth taking care of Naomi, I think of my mom who sacrificed three years of her life to take care of my grandparents while they lived with my parents. She cooked, cleaned, waited in doctor's offices, talked to social security agents, bathed, blotted wounds, played cards, shuttled to church, hauled oxygen tanks, divvied pills, cried, perused the library for murder mysteries and autobiographies, pep-talked, folded laundry, played more cards, and on and on. Her sacrifice was rarely applauded or appreciated, though not a moment was missed under God's gaze.

Perhaps some of you have also been in long seasons of unnoticed hard work, sacrifice, and faithfulness. We wonder if our stories will ever make it to the ears of a Boaz—a boss, a pastor, or a future spouse. To God. I am reminded today that Boaz seeing Ruth was God seeing her, and He sees you too. Let's take a look at some of God's promises to the obedient and faithful in heart.

READ ISAIAH 58:6-12. What did God promise the Israelites who took care of their own flesh and blood, fed the poor, helped the oppressed, and fought against injustice (vv. 8-11)?

READ GALATIANS 6:9. Why did Paul tell the Galatians not to give up in doing good?

READ HEBREWS 6:10. What will God not forget?

PERSONAL REFLECTION: How do these verses encourage you today?

God was not unfaithful in forgetting Ruth's labor of love, nor will He be unfaithful in forgetting yours. As we close, I want to circle back to something we touched on at the beginning of today's study. Verse 10 quotes Ruth saying to Boaz, "Why have I found such favor in your eyes that you notice me—a foreigner?" (NIV). There's a pun in the original language that can be translated as something along the lines of, "You have noticed the unnoticed" or "recognized the unrecognized."[1] Ruth's response reveals the vulnerability she felt as a non-Israelite, not to mention what she felt as a woman in a field where men may have wanted to take advantage of her.[2] Her survival was based on the goodwill of Israelite farmers, but Boaz went well beyond helping her survive. Daniel I. Block says, "Boaz had dignified this destitute widow from a foreign land and treated her as a significant person, on par socially with his hired and presumably Israelite field workers."[3]

We must give credit to Boaz for such immense kindness, but we also must see that ultimately God is the One who was behind the favor Ruth was shown. He notices the unnoticeable. He gives favor to the foreigner. He lifts up the downtrodden.

> God notices the unnoticeable. He gives favor to the foreigner. He lifts up the downtrodden.

PERSONAL REFLECTION: What has today's Scripture taught you about the heart of God? What about it feels specifically different than the limitations and biases of human love?

We're not done seeing God's favor and heart for the vulnerable expressed through Boaz. God's unconditional love and kindness will shine more brightly with each turning page. If you are in humble circumstances, weary of a world that prizes beauty over substance, or quietly serving others in the shadows, may you experience God's favor upon you in fresh ways today.

DAY 2
UNDER HIS WINGS

Only God
could pull
off the
divine gift of
redemption.

I always enjoy when the Old Testament gives us New Testament glimpses. In my humble opinion, today's passage of Scripture includes one of the more prominent pictures of the gospel found in the Old Testament. We're in for an encouraging day of study. Especially for the downtrodden soul longing for refuge.

READ RUTH 2:10-13. We'll include yesterday's reading for context.

What other name besides "LORD" did Boaz call God in verse 12?

God of _____.

Why is this name significant considering Ruth was a Moabitess?

PERSONAL TAKE: What does this tell you about God's heart for the nations that surrounded Israel?

Despite Boaz's power and wealth, he knew the limitations of his resources and abilities. Boaz could offer water, grain, and protection, but only God could pull off the divine gift of redemption. Although Boaz was exceptionally capable and resourced, he knew his limitations.

I think it's significant that Ruth found refuge in the God of Israel before she found it in the strong arms of Boaz. I have often looked for safe harbor in people before seeking it in Christ. I have repeatedly learned the hard way that the best of humans are limited. As years have matured me and my relationship with Jesus has deepened, my soul really does long for the shelter and shadow of His wings. And as situations arise that find me looking for fulfillment in another person, those become opportunities for me to seek His shelter and listen to His voice.

Ruth is not the only one to have found shelter under the wings of Yahweh. Read the following psalms and reflect on their meanings by responding to each corresponding question.

> READ PSALM 36:7. What does taking refuge under the shadow of God's wings look like for you?

Ruth found refuge in the God of Israel before she found it in the strong arms of Boaz.

> READ PSALM 61:4. List some specific ways refuge in God's tent differs from the temporary places we look for safety and stability.

> READ PSALM 91:1-4. How did the psalmist describe the intimacy of taking refuge in God? Write down all the words and phrases you notice.

Let's briefly turn to the New Testament to hear Jesus speak to those He came to redeem.

> READ MATTHEW 23:37. How is Jesus's language similar to what you just read in Ruth and Psalms?

Jesus longs to take us under His wings. And yet we often resist Him and look instead for temporary shelters or passing places of shade.

PERSONAL REFLECTION: In what inadequate shelters are you trying to find refuge? What has been the result?

PRAYER: Pray a prayer that seeks to take refuge in Christ. Here is an example to get you started: *Heavenly Father, through Christ You are calling me to rest in the shadow of Your almighty wings. I confess that I look to the strong and resourced, the handsome and nurturing, the temporary shelters that feel familiar. Even when they fail and disappoint me, I return. But this is not where I want to make my home. I want my dwelling place to be under Your wings, where Your presence is known, and I am secure. May Jesus be greater to me than all others. Amen.*

REREAD RUTH 2:13. What does Ruth commend Boaz for?

Boaz "comforted" and consoled Ruth. The Hebrew can mean to allay one's fears, which absolutely ministers to me.[4] The second expression, translated *encouraged* (CSB) or *spoken kindly* (ESV) literally means "to speak on the heart" and has to do with words of compassion and sympathy.[5]

PERSONAL REFLECTION: There is something special about the kind and compassionate words we speak. Take a moment to think of someone you can speak a word of kindness to this week. Write his or her name here: _____. What will you tell that person? Make a plan to talk in person or write a note.

In verse 13, Boaz's kindness surprised Ruth because she was (circle your answer):

A Moabitess   A widow

Beneath a servant girl   A woman

Not only did Ruth not qualify as one of the servant girls, but she was also beneath them. Ruth viewed her status in society as lower than the lowest rung on the ladder. This truth blessed me during a humbling time in my life. It reminded me that humble circumstances don't have to equate to humiliation. Ruth acknowledged her standing in society yet appeared unashamed. She expressed her gratitude for Boaz's kindness and didn't harden her spirit by bitter wallowing or feeling sorry for herself. We don't know all that she was dealing with internally or how she kept a positive attitude, but it's clear God used her humble state to prepare her for what lay ahead.

PERSONAL TAKE: Given what you know of the story so far, how might Ruth benefit from the humble path she was forced to walk in her present moment?

When I was in college, I had a sociology textbook that listed every known profession from most prestigious to most humbling. I can't remember what stood at the top, but I can't forget what the author concluded was at the bottom: shoe shining. I couldn't wait to tell my dad because before he started the church he pastored for forty-seven years, he gave golf lessons, and yes, shined people's shoes. He now realizes those years of sitting at people's feet with a well-worn rag and pitch-black polish were not all that far from what God was preparing him to do for the rest of his life—serve Christ's body.

As we close today, let me encourage you to not resist the path of humility. When God has ordained the humbling, you can be wholly certain His love is the catalyst, and the process is forming in you a meek and gentle heart, preparing you for the abundance ahead. If you feel like God has you in the place of a servant girl—or even beneath one—humble yourself under His mighty hand. In due time He will lift you up.

He raises the poor from the dust and lifts the needy from the trash heap in order to seat them with nobles—with the nobles of his people. He gives the childless woman a household, making her the joyful mother of children. Hallelujah!

PSALM 113:7-9

DAY 3
INVITED TO THE TABLE

My dining room table is my home's place of nourishment and belonging.

My dining room table is long and slender with a flat edge on one end and an arc on the other like an old church door. I found it in an antique shop south of Nashville. The tag said it was more than one hundred years old and hailed from a church in Connecticut. I wonder if any of this is true or if they just saw me coming. I fell in love the moment I saw it. My sister Katie took down the dimensions, and within an hour I'd rented a truck and off we drove with the brand new super old table. It's one of my favorite pieces in my house. Long enough for a substantial dinner party but thin enough for everyone to feel closely knit. It's my home's place of nourishment and belonging, which is one reason why today's reading feels so special to me.

READ RUTH 2:10-14. Once again, I'm including previous verses as a reminder of context.

We don't know how much time passed between Ruth's closing response in verse 13 and Boaz's invitation to a meal in verse 14. The pause helps us appreciate the echo of Ruth's words still hanging in the air—her status is less than that of a slave girl. And it serves to highlight the extraordinary invitation Boaz was about to extend, one that far exceeded what the law required. Suddenly, Ruth found herself sitting at Boaz's table, not among the gleaners but among the reapers!

A lot of detail is packed into verse 14. List each detail in your own words.

PERSONAL TAKE: What element or gesture from verse 14 strikes you as most meaningful and why?

In the Ancient Near East, eating together wasn't merely about nourishment, it also held great symbolic significance.[6] Meals expressed hospitality, celebration, sometimes even solidifying deals between parties.[7] Old Testament scholar Daniel I. Block expresses Boaz's gesture in meaningful terms, "Obviously this verse is not simply about feeding the hungry. The narrator hereby shows how Boaz took an ordinary occasion and transformed it into a glorious demonstration of compassion, generosity, and acceptance—in short, the biblical understanding of *ḥeseḏ*."[8]

PERSONAL TAKE: How did Boaz's invitation to his table dignify Ruth in a way that surpassed the mere offer of food?

Ruth mentioned her status as below that of a servant girl (v. 13), and in the very next verse, she found herself sitting beside the harvesters. Perhaps her words had rung in Boaz's ears. Perhaps he remembered the goodness of God to the poor and outcast (Deut. 24:19-22) and decided that he too wanted to be a man after God's heart. He treated Ruth not as a lowly slave girl but as part of his family.[9]

This part of Ruth's story reminds me of a future story of King David and the astonishing kindness he showed to a young man named Mephibosheth.

READ 2 SAMUEL 9:1-12. (This event took place after the death of Jonathan, King David's dearest friend.)

List all the similarities you can find between Ruth and Boaz's story and Mephibosheth and David's story.

We all long to be invited to the table. It represents belonging, acceptance, honor, and chosenness. It offers intimacy, conversation, nourishment, and safety. Typically, though, we invite people like ourselves to our tables. How often do we look to welcome the lonely newcomer, the unbeliever who doesn't share our convictions, the foreigner whose customs are different from ours, or the person who can't offer us anything in return? Jesus spoke to this very issue in a passage from Luke's Gospel.

READ LUKE 14:12-14. Why did Jesus tell the Pharisees and their friends to invite the poor instead of those they normally hung out with?

What do we learn about how God views the poor, sick, and outcast from Jesus's instructions here?

PERSONAL REFLECTION: What's a specific way you can use your home or table to more closely reflect the heart of Christ based on today's study? Who can you reach out to and offer a place of nourishment and conversation?

What was remarkable about Ruth being invited to Boaz's table and Mephibosheth having a place at David's table is that neither were societally worthy. Neither had means of entrance. Each had to be invited by a person who was not only powerful and resourced but also generous and kind. Even Jesus, while admonishing those around Him to invite the lowly to their banquets, was seated beside sinners. His coming to eat with those He came to save was not only sacrifice; it was love. If Jesus showed such merciful love at the table, shouldn't we also?

BACK TO RUTH 2:14. After Ruth ate and was satisfied, what additional detail is given? What additional insight does this give us into the heart of God reflected in Boaz?

We belong to a generous and lavish God who desires to give good gifts to His children (Matt. 7:11). Even in seasons of leanness, we can trust His heart toward us, assured His provision comes in different forms. The past several years I've had a certain void in my life that I haven't been able to permanently fill. I look around and others seem to have this provision in spades. It doesn't seem like God is dealing generously with me here. In fact, it seems as though He's withholding. I've occasionally despaired over this gap in my life. Sometimes I've been angry. But I always find myself back at His table, sitting in the company of His children. Taking my place not because I have the means but because I am loved. And I'm learning that even when certain provisions feel scarce, He is more generous than I often thank Him for being.

I want to leave you with a passage in Revelation about a remarkable feast that is yet to come, a picture of Jesus's table, the ultimate place of nourishment and belonging.

READ WHAT REVELATION 19:6-10 SAYS ABOUT THIS FEAST.
According to verse 9, who is blessed?

At the wedding feast of the Lamb, what will Christ's bride be wearing (vv. 7-8)?

What do these garments stand for (v. 8)? Circle your answer.

Cumulative Bible knowledge   Money we've tithed

The righteous acts of the saints   The prayers of the righteous

The church (the bride of Christ) has made herself ready by wearing fine linens that represent the righteousness (righteous acts) of the saints. At first glance, this almost looks like getting to Christ's table is a matter of living the best life we possibly can, hoping that in the end our outfit will be white and clean enough to inherit heaven. How grateful I am for verse 8:

FILL IN THE BLANK USING THE CSB TRANSLATION: "She was _____ fine linen to wear, bright and pure."

The linen has been given to us to wear! It is not up to us to clothe ourselves in our own self-righteousness. Jesus Christ is our righteousness. The good news of the gospel is that Jesus has extended an invitation to every one of us.

You may be thinking: *But you don't know my past.* Part of what makes the gospel good news is that nothing in our lives is too scarlet to be covered by the white linen of His righteousness. Though we are unworthy, we are invited to God's table because of Christ's kindness and authority.

PERSONAL RESPONSE: If you've already accepted the linens of righteousness, write words of thanks to Christ for such a remarkable gift.

Nothing in our lives is too scarlet to be covered by the white linen of Christ's righteousness.

If this is a new truth that you've never understood before, today is the day to be clothed in Christ's righteousness. On page 188, there is a much broader explanation of what Jesus has done for you. Take time to read about His immeasurable love for you.

Like Mephibosheth, we are crippled in both feet; like Ruth, we bear the stain of Moab; like Boaz, we are limited by our human frame. We all need the Son of God.

Dearest Jesus,
This gift is too amazing to fathom, too lavish to take in. Like Ruth and Mephibosheth, we gladly come to Your table knowing it is only because of You we are invited. Like Boaz, we recognize that only under Your wing will any of us ever find refuge (Ruth 2:12). The power and kindness of Boaz and David were extraordinary, but they had no power to forgive sins, no authority to clothe in righteousness. These gifts only come by the power of God through the kindness of Christ. We love You and thank You.
Amen.

DAY 4
A GENEROUS GIFT

Another wonderful passage of Ruth lies ahead of us today. My prayer is that as we continue to follow the trail of Boaz's generosity it will lead us straight to the feet of Christ. Take the reading slow and do your best to put yourself in Ruth's position. Consider her hopes, her fears, her emotions.

READ RUTH 2:14-17.

What did Boaz tell his workers to do regarding Ruth, and what did he tell them not to do? Fill in the blanks below.

Let her _____
_____ and don't
_____(v. 15).

Pull out _____

_____
and don't _____ (v. 16).

HOLD YOUR PLACE IN RUTH AND LOOK UP DEUTERONOMY 24:17-22. How did Boaz's instructions go beyond what the law required?

What did God twice tell the Israelites to remember (vv. 18,22)?

PERSONAL TAKE: Why do you think this was significant for Israel to remember?

If Boaz had merely held to the letter of God's law, then he would have allowed Ruth to glean in his field and that would have been the end of it. But I have to believe Boaz understood the heartbeat of this Deuteronomy

> My prayer is that as we continue to follow the trail of Boaz's generosity it will lead us straight to the feet of Christ.

When God's love is the backdrop of His commands, suddenly there are no limits on the love and generosity Boaz was to show Ruth.

passage and that it had to do with God's deliverance of Israel. God commanded the Israelites to be kind and generous to the foreigner, widow, and fatherless because God was kind and generous to them in delivering them from Egypt. When God's love is the backdrop of His commands, suddenly there are no limits on the love and generosity Boaz was to show Ruth.

CONTINUE TO HOLD YOUR PLACE IN RUTH AND READ MATTHEW 22:34-40.

What two commands do all the law and the prophets hang upon?

PERSONAL REFLECTION: Consider Boaz's actions toward Ruth and Jesus's teaching on love. Is there an area of your life where you're going through religious motions instead of serving or obeying out of love? Give this some thought.

Before we continue, I want to emphasize the foreshadowing of the gospel in today's Ruth passage. We often think that the law was about rules and Christ was about love, but God's law has always been about love. Boaz demonstrates his understanding of this. Oh, that we might be gripped by the overwhelming redemption of Christ so that every command we obey is born out of love for God and love for others. Only then will we see lives changed for God's glory.

CONTINUE READING RUTH 2:17-18. How much grain did Ruth carry back to town?

Scholars believe an *ephah* (twenty-six quarts) was between thirty and fifty pounds.[10] Regardless of the exact weight, this was an astounding amount of grain to take home after only one day's work. Ruth wisely took full advantage of Boaz's offer to safely glean in his fields. She would not leave blessing and provision ungathered.

True/False: According to verse 18, Ruth shared what she'd gathered with Naomi.

LOOK BACK AT RUTH 1:21. What are some specific ways you see God contradicting Naomi's perception that He brought her back empty?

PERSONAL REFLECTION: How does Naomi's misperception about God encourage you to view Him as He is revealed in Scripture versus letting your circumstances dictate your feelings about Him? How can you apply this to a specific circumstance in your life?

Ruth's work ethic continued to shine. Though Boaz's workers left sheaves for her to gather, she still had to do the work of picking them up, threshing what was gathered, and carrying the grain back into town. These were long, physically taxing days. Her generosity to Naomi is equally inspiring. She shared out of what she was given as well as what she earned.

I want to close with two portions of Paul's second letter to the Corinthians. These verses will shed further light on what we've reflected on today.

READ 2 CORINTHIANS 8:1-5,9.

For context, Paul was encouraging the church in Corinth to take up a collection for the struggling Jewish community. In this passage, he referenced how the churches in Macedonia were faithful to give.

True/False:

_____ The Macedonian churches gave out of their extreme poverty.

_____ They gave as much as they were able and no more.

_____ They saw giving as a painful hardship but did it anyway (v. 4).

I've been self-employed my entire adult life. I've been through years where work was sparse, and I've also enjoyed surprise abundance. Even during times when I was broken, depressed, and depleted, God wanted me to give. And I'm not only talking about money. He wanted me to share my time, resources, wisdom, instruction, comfort, labor, and so on.

PERSONAL RESPONSE: How might you give out of your wealth? How might you give out of what feels like a lean season?

TURN OVER A FEW PAGES AND READ 2 CORINTHIANS 9:6-11.

If we sow sparingly, we will reap _____.

If we sow generously, we will reap _____.

Close by writing out 2 Corinthians 9:8 in the space provided.

We all have something to give even if we're broke or broken.

For much of this week's study, we've focused on the generosity of Boaz who gave out of his wealth, but today we saw Ruth, much like the Macedonian churches, give out of her poverty. We all have something to give even if we're broke or broken. Ruth refused to wear the cloak of lowly, foreign, bereft servant girl who had nothing to offer. These labels may have been true of her cultural experience, but they didn't define her. She had the humility to receive from Boaz's hand and the strength to turn around and bless someone else. Oh, that we might aspire to humility that can receive another's blessing, mingled with the God-given dignity that assures we always have something to offer.

PERSONAL RESPONSE: Think of one way you can give to someone today and write it down.

DAY 5
A KINSMAN-REDEEMER

We couldn't have picked a better section of Ruth to end the week. Today we're going to find out information that changes the course of this story. Our hearts will be stirred by a redeemer—not the One whose birth and resurrection we celebrate every year, but a foreshadowing of Him. A human redeemer with the power to restore lives but not souls, whose extraordinary *hesed* could change earthly destinies but not eternal ones. He will bless and inspire us, but mostly he will make us yearn for the ultimate Redeemer, Jesus Christ.

> Boaz will bless us and inspire us, but mostly he will make us yearn for the ultimate Redeemer, Jesus Christ.

READ RUTH 2:19-23.

When Naomi saw the amount of grain and leftover food Ruth had brought her, what did she ask Ruth (v. 19)?

How did Ruth answer?

Naomi asked Ruth where she had worked, but Ruth wanted her to know with *whom* she'd worked.[11] Ruth told Naomi, "The name of the man I worked with today is Boaz" (v. 19). It was a person more than a place who changed Ruth's life.

We can get easily sidetracked by emphasizing the places where our ministries to others take place—*How elaborate is the setup? How many programs are offered? What systems are in place to help us carry out our work?* But this brief exchange between Naomi and Ruth is a reminder that lives are primarily touched by other lives. All the other trappings are a far second. For Ruth, the important thing wasn't where she gleaned but who had given her the opportunity. Boaz noticed her, spoke tenderly to her, invited her to his table, offered protection, and gave of his resources.

PERSONAL RESPONSE: How can you be a "who" to someone? In other words, with whom can you invest your time, not just your gifts?

I would have loved to witness the interaction of Ruth telling Naomi she'd worked that day with Boaz. After the grueling losses and years of displacement in Moab, just hearing that name in connection with Ruth's must have been surreal for Naomi. A bit of hope was finally on the horizon.

According to verse 20, whom did Naomi say Boaz was?

He's a close relative and a _____.

Up to this point, Ruth knew Boaz to be a powerful, kind, and generous landowner who enabled her to provide for herself and Naomi. But that last detail alters the course of the story. For ancient-day listeners, the revelation of Boaz as one of Naomi's family redeemers (different translations may say "guardian-redeemer" or just "redeemer") would have caught their attention.

The concept of a family redeemer comes from the Hebrew term *gō'ēl*, which means kinsman-redeemer.[12] To best understand the function of a kinsman-redeemer, we need to look at a few Old Testament passages that deal with Israelite family law. You were hoping for this excursion, I know.

READ LEVITICUS 25:25. What is a kinsman-redeemer allowed to do in this situation?

READ LEVITICUS 25:47-49. What is a kinsman-redeemer allowed to do in this situation?

READ DEUTERONOMY 25:5-10. What is the brother-in-law obliged to do in this situation? *(Note: This is called Levirate marriage. It came into play when a widow was without children and her brother-in-law married her so as to carry on the family name and legacy of her deceased husband. This obligation doesn't deal expressly with the duty of a kinsman-redeemer, but it's a part of the law that will be important to our story later.)*

We find in other portions of the law that the *gō'ēl* could go after restitution money on behalf of a relative who died as a result of a crime (Num. 5:7-8) and could ensure that justice was served (Ps. 119:153-154; Jer. 50:33-34).[13] To summarize, the *gō'ēl* was the near relative who was to ensure the economic well-being of a relative, and was especially instrumental when that person was incapable of getting himself or herself out of the crisis.[14] "The custom of redemption was designed to maintain the wholeness and health of family relationships, even after the person has died."[15]

God in His wisdom wrote these instructions and provisions into His law to protect and preserve the weak. Remember how defenseless a woman with no husband would have been at that time in a patriarchal society. The provision of the *gō'ēl* (kinsman-redeemer) was all about family—for an Israelite, no one should ever be alone, destitute, or without the hope of having a family legacy.

> Now that you know more about the function and purpose of a *gō'ēl*, or kinsman-redeemer, how does Boaz being a close relative revive the story line so far?

In Ruth 2:20 Naomi said, "May the Lᴏʀᴅ bless him because he has not abandoned his kindness to the living or the dead." It's not clear whether the "he" in this sentence is referring to Boaz or to God. Either way, we can credit God as ultimately showing kindness, whether directly to the women or through Boaz. What's significant is that the word *kindness* here is used to translate the important word *ḥesed*. Remember that *ḥesed* is one of the most powerful phrases of covenant love and loyalty in the Hebrew language, and it plays an important role in the book of Ruth.

We can tell by Naomi's phrasing that she had assumed God abandoned such covenant loyalty to her and her family. She seems surprised to discover He had not abandoned His covenant after all.

What reasons did Naomi give for thinking God abandoned His covenant of loyalty and love to her?

PERSONAL REFLECTION: What circumstances in your life cause you to question God's commitment and promises to you? Is this something you've questioned recently?

READ PSALM 31:22. What conclusion did the psalmist jump to and why?

LOOK BACK AT RUTH 2:22-23. How long had Ruth been given work and provision for?

COMPARE RUTH 1:22 AND 2:23. Record your observations about how God was at work in Naomi's and Ruth's lives.

In my alarm I said, "I am cut off from your sight." But you heard the sound of my pleading when I cried to you for help.

PSALM 31:22

Prior to Ruth 2:19, Naomi was aware she had a kinsman-redeemer named Boaz but didn't know Ruth had met him; Ruth knew Boaz but didn't know he was a kinsman-redeemer of her father-in-law's family. In verses 19-20, these pieces of information collide and not only change the direction of the story but also remind us that our God does not forsake His promises toward us. In this part of the story, we get a glimpse of the fullness and totality of God's provision in the lives of His children.

As we close this week's study, I want to set our sights on the full and ultimate redemption bestowed on us in Christ, to which the book of Ruth points.

READ GALATIANS 3:10-14 AND 4:1-7.

PERSONAL RESPONSE: As a result of studying the Old Testament law of redemption, in what new way(s) do you understand Jesus's redemption of you?

May our hearts grow with deeper appreciation for our one true Redeemer, Jesus, the most unique of all.

One reason I want you to understand the *gō'ēl* in Scripture* is because it helps us further understand not just Boaz but how Jesus has uniquely redeemed us. As we become further enamored with Boaz, so our hearts will grow with deeper appreciation for our one true Redeemer, Jesus, the most unique of all.

No doubt we've covered a lot of ground this session, though perhaps not as wide as deep. Digging into Old Testament law, peeking into Revelation, reading about people with names like Mephibosheth, enduring a study on humility, and committing to give more are not for the timid. I'm really honored to take this journey with you. We're at the halfway point, and the best is still to come.

*Note: If you'd like to study more about the kinsman-redeemer's role, here are several passages: Leviticus 25:25-30; Leviticus 25:47-55; Numbers 5:8; Numbers 35:12,19-27; Job 19:25; Psalm 119:154; Jeremiah 50:34.[16]

WATCH

WATCH the Session Four video teaching and take notes below.

To access the video teaching sessions, use the instructions in the back of your Bible study book.

RAINBOW SALAD

Salads have gotten fancy. I don't know when this happened, but gone are the days of the plain salad. I like this one because it brings a lot of color and is a hearty meal in itself. It lets people know you tried. If you need to impress or if you just need something healthy and substantial, this is a great choice.

(SERVES 4–6)

INGREDIENTS FOR SALAD

1 cup of baby greens
1 cup of arugula
½ cup of purple cabbage, chopped
½ cup of quinoa, cooked and cooled
½ cup of red onion, chopped
1 garlic clove, chopped
1 cup of red cherry tomatoes cut in half
½ cup of chickpeas, cooked and rinsed
½ cup of lentils, cooked
⅓ cup of cucumber, chopped
Juice of one lemon

INGREDIENTS FOR VINAIGRETTE

¼ cup of balsamic vinegar
Zest of one lemon
2 tablespoons chopped parsley
1 garlic clove, minced
½ teaspoon of dijon mustard
3 tablespoons of olive oil
Salt and pepper to taste
¼ teaspoon of sugar

DIRECTIONS

1. Toss the salad ingredients together and dress with vinaigrette.

2. Serve with some toasted pita bread triangles.

 Turn to pages 184–187 for appetizer, side, and dessert ideas that go well with this dish.

A PROPOSAL

Occasionally my work travels take me to some of the more desirable parts of the country—the jagged crags of the northeast overlooking the Atlantic, a seafood house in South Beach, and one of my favorites for a thousand reasons, New York City. On one particular trip, I landed in sunny LA near the end of January, which is my favorite time to speak in Southern California because Nashville is a lot of things in January, but warm and sunny is not one of them.

My friend and I zipped off in our snazzy rental car—you know, a Volkswagen®—and headed straight for the LA Farmers Market. For some odd reason, I had never made that stop before. Now having experienced it, I can't explain the travesty of this oversight. For me, cooking is reverie, and I adore eating. All that fresh produce and exotic vendors coming together in one place under a single roof was like stepping into my best daydream. After a fabulous Singapore soup with homemade *roti paratha* (a type of bread like I'd never tasted), we were off to Beverly Hills.

Beverly Hills is an obligatory stop, simply because it's Beverly Hills. I mostly wanted to go there because it's where my grandmother grew up and I wanted to see her childhood home. And possibly Tom Hanks. She lived there in the '20s and '30s, and her address still exists. My friend and I drove up to the front of the house as the owner was getting out of her very expensive car. I almost waved her down to tell her about my grandmother, but then I also thought about the possibility of going to Beverly Hills jail for stalking and decided to keep driving.

The next day we arrived at the church where I was speaking. It was a special group of people, one of those experiences that stays with you. The staff was thoughtful and kind, and the nearly seven hundred women were encouraging and intent on

Some places we can only go with God by ourselves.

learning. I taught three times from Jesus's Sermon on the Mount, and we finished the event with a Q&R (question and response). The women's ministry director made her way through a pile of questions scribbled on note cards. Eventually, we got to the one I always get in these settings, the question I dread, the one I will get as long as I am without a husband: *How do you deal with being single?*

Partly because I don't dread singleness, I never know how to answer that question. Every person's story is different. And every decade of singleness presents different types of loneliness, challenges, and opportunities. In my twenties and early thirties, I really grieved not having that one person to go through life with. I also lamented not having children. Now that I'm in my forties, that biological ship has sailed; its finality is both more sad and more freeing. Until recently, I never thought much about the term *set in one's ways*, but at this point, I'm committed to what side of the bed I sleep on and the temperature the thermostat is set to, and I'm used to coming and going without checking in with too many people.

I'd like to think of myself as free and flexible and not set in my ways, but the reality is I am crystallizing to some degree. Would I be willing to blow some of this up for falling in love with a wonderful man? I think so. But this hasn't yet happened, so I live with an undeserved amount of community and joy and nieces and nephews and family members around the corner, along with the void of not having my own husband, my own children, or the makings of a biological legacy. Each of us works to balance our own assortment of blessings and longings.

So I suppose the question of how I deal with singleness is answered similarly to how do any of us deal with any kind of ongoing challenge or trial. God meets us along the way, sometimes unmistakably and at other times in a more imperceptible fashion, but always with us, changing us, refining us, proving Himself sufficient. God's activity in our lives is on mighty display in this week's study. Without prematurely unveiling the details, Ruth will bear her grief, longings, and hope to the threshing floor under the canopy of night, alone. Some places we can only go with God by ourselves. And once Ruth gets to the threshing floor, there will be no guarantees. She has been promised nothing. Her venture is not a demand on God, *If I do this, God, then You must do that*. Instead, she appears to go out of obedience, no strings attached, only expectation in Almighty God. This is the way we must approach our own threshing floors. Without demands. Sometimes in the dark. But always with the expectation that God will be there, faithful and good.

This will be our most personal week so far if we're willing to open our hearts. There are great rewards at the threshing floor—not rewards we necessarily get to handpick, but ones God chooses for us that are beyond our imagination.

MAY THE LORD BLESS YOU, MY DAUGHTER.

Ruth 3:10

DAY 1
A MOTHER-IN-LAW'S REQUEST

Discovering a
solution to
a problem
doesn't mean
we don't
have to wait
for things to
change.

Some portions of Scripture require a certain amount of gearing up for. We have to ready our minds for complex theological truths in sections of Paul's letters. We gird our emotions for the famines, desolation, and exilic listlessness in parts of the prophetic books. But then there are those passages that fluff the sunken love seat for us and hand us a cup of tea. They spread a blanket over us and invite us in for a love story. A hope story. Ah, yes, a gospel story.

BEGIN BY READING ALL OF RUTH 2.

> How long did Ruth glean in Boaz's field, and with whom did she live during that time?

A good bit of time passed between Naomi and Ruth's conversation about Boaz being their *gō'ēl* (vv. 19-22) and Ruth finishing the barley and wheat harvests (v. 23). This would have been from about late April to early June. Though Naomi and Ruth had discovered the good news of Boaz as their *gō'ēl*, life didn't immediately turn around. We can all relate. Discovering a solution to a problem doesn't necessarily mean we don't have to wait for things to change.

Perhaps it's not coincidental that as I write, my own work is changing and I'm not sure of what's ahead. I'm home a lot more than I used to be. My next endeavors might look a bit different than my previous ones. I have a healthy unrest and unknowing but also an expectation that God is leading me through this in-between time of working and waiting. Today's reminder encourages me, and I hope it does you too.

> **READ RUTH 3:1-6.** How did Naomi address Ruth in verse 1? Circle your answer.
>
> My friend   My daughter-in-law
>
> My daughter   My dear
>
> True/False: In verse 2, Naomi said, "Boaz is my relative"?

This is the second time Naomi referred to Boaz as a redeemer of "ours" (2:20; 3:2). That, combined with Naomi's description of Ruth as "my daughter," shows us Naomi now recognized Ruth as part of her Israelite family.

PERSONAL TAKE: Look back at Ruth 1:11-13 and compare Naomi's past words to her present ones. What do you think brought about these changes? How does this speak to her change of heart?

PERSONAL REFLECTION: Look back at Ruth 1:8-9. I wonder if Naomi ever thought she would be the answer to her own prayer for Ruth. Is it possible that God is asking you to be part of the answer to a prayer you've been praying for another person? Journal your thoughts.

There's no question that Ruth's loyal and relentless love toward Naomi helped to sweeten her bitterness and quell her hopelessness. Ruth worked her way into Naomi's heart through loyalty, consistency, and self-sacrifice. This should give us hope for even the hardest people we've been called to love.

PERSONAL RESPONSE: Who are you having difficulty loving right now? What are some specific actions and attitudes you can emulate in Ruth? (As you think about this, keep in mind the power of the Holy Spirit. The love of Christ and the fruit of the Spirit through you will be what make a difference.)

Naomi and Ruth's relationship will continue to offer us hope for our own ailing relationships, but for now, we're heading to the threshing floor. It is our duty to go where the story leads, and what drama awaits us there. We must spend ample time considering things like Naomi's scheming—remarks like, *Now, isn't Boaz our relative?* as if it's the first time she's thought of this—and Ruth's new outfit and fresh scent, the fact that it's nighttime, oh so many things to discuss.

List Naomi's instructions to Ruth in the order they were given.

How many of Naomi's instructions did Ruth carry out (3:6)?

After completing Naomi's instructions, what was Ruth to wait for (v. 4)?

Since some of these details in verse 3 are culturally specific, let's consider each one.

Washing and perfuming. This was meant to accomplish what you might think. The intent was for Ruth to be her most attractive and presentable. My mom once surprised me with a sampler of my favorite brand of perfumes for Christmas. Somehow a few sprays make me feel more feminine, more myself. The right scent is magical.

Best clothes/dress. My nieces and I watched a movie where the lead female character was sent an invitation to a dance. The card ended with the phrase "formal attire." I explained that phrase to my niece Harper, which incidentally needed little explanation when the lead showed up in a gorgeous ball gown. Harper was smitten with the puff sleeves and flowing fabric. It's tempting to think Ruth went to the threshing floor in formal attire, but the Hebrew word *śimlâ* simply means an outer garment that covers the whole body except the head.[1] Despite certain translations, there doesn't appear to be anything extra fancy about this clothing. What's significant, though, is the idea that Ruth changed into new clothes. We'll talk more about this important point tomorrow.

The threshing floor. This is an interesting place for Naomi to have sent Ruth, especially at night. This was not like sending her to singles' pizza night at the local church. In ancient Israel, especially during winnowing season, the threshing floor was often linked with sexual activity. Since men would sleep next to their piles of grain, prostitutes knew this to be a place where they could offer their services, making it a compromising and suggestive environment (Hos. 9:1).[2]

Eating and drinking. In addition to the precarious nature of time and place, Naomi told Ruth to go to Boaz after he had something to eat and drink. More than likely this drink was alcoholic, though it seems unlikely from everything else the text tells us about Boaz that he would have drunk excessively.

Uncover his feet. This is a difficult image for modern-day readers to make sense of. Scholars have wondered about it meaning everything from uncovering sexual organs to nakedness to his actual feet. Because nothing in the book of Ruth indicates anything other than Ruth, Boaz, and Naomi being God-fearing Israelites of character, we can go with the assumption that Ruth was to uncover his actual feet. Nonetheless, Ruth lying down at Boaz's uncovered feet was still a vulnerable and suggestive position for both.

All of these elements add up to a scenario where a lot could go wrong. Ruth could have easily been mistaken for a Moabite prostitute; Boaz could have been appalled by her forwardness and rejected her advances; they could have engaged in sexual behavior which would have gone against God's law. "After all, the events described occur in the dark days of the judges."[3]

Scholar Daniel I. Block's comments about this scene are worth including in full:

> From a natural perspective the desired response was actually the least likely to occur. What are the chances that Boaz will wake up and in his groggy state notice that Ruth has covered herself with a *śimlâ* rather than the seductive garb of a prostitute, that he will understand when she introduces herself, that he will respond favorably toward her, overlooking the irregularities of the situation (a woman proposing to a man, a younger person proposing to an older, a field worker proposing to the field owner, an alien proposing to a native), and that, in fulfillment of Naomi's words, he will give Ruth rational instructions concerning how to proceed? But by this time Naomi's faith is strong. She has confidence in Boaz's integrity and apparently in the hidden hand of God to govern his reactions when he awakes.
>
> Remarkably, Ruth's faith appears to be equal to that of her mother-in-law, for she gives herself wholly to carrying out Naomi's scheme in full. Meanwhile the narrator challenges the reader to trust God the way these women do. The first scene closes, leaving us to wonder if this delicate and dangerous plan will work.[4]

śimlâ:
an outer garment that covered virtually the entire body except the head

My opinion is that Naomi was an honorable woman who didn't intend to promote promiscuous behavior between Ruth and Boaz. To me, her intentions seem born out of a desire to see someone love and care for Ruth. Perhaps, though, in her zeal to accomplish something very good, she may have put Ruth and Boaz in a compromising situation that could have upended both of their lives. Again, this is just my personal take. I may tend to see it this way because I've often tried to accomplish good things by going about them in the wrong way. So maybe I'm projecting on Naomi. I would love to know how you've assimilated these details. No matter what we think of Naomi's plot, one of the most remarkable and mysterious parts of life is how God takes our frail and human plans and weaves them into His master plan. The wisdom of Scripture sums this up best.

Next to each verse, write a brief description of God's ultimate sovereignty over our plans.

Proverbs 16:1

Proverbs 20:24

Proverbs 21:30-31

Jeremiah 10:23

We sometimes mistakenly think our lives are solely up to us and any plan or decision we get wrong will have cascading consequences. But this is to miss experiencing the confidence and peace Jesus gives. We won't get every decision right. We will make mistakes, and sometimes we may even sin in our attempts to do what we think is right. But God is sovereign over the steps we take.

PERSONAL RESPONSE: How do the truths of these verses help you trade stress and anxiety for God's peace and rest?

As you continue to reflect on Ruth's journey to the threshing floor, think about what it would mean to let your defenses down. The ones that keep you from hoping because you can't bear to be disappointed again. Be blessed today that God's supremacy and providence reign over all your plans. He is the One who directs your steps. Are you willing to trust Him?

DAY 2
A NEW DAY

Today's study is deeply personal as we look at the risk and symbolism involved in Ruth's visit to the threshing floor at night. Yesterday we took a closer look at the foreign practices Ruth undertook. Now we'll look at what might have been going on in her heart as she followed Naomi's instructions.

As a foreigner, widow, woman, and servant girl, Ruth's trek to the threshing floor held plenty of uncertainty. While we probably can't relate to her exact journey, I imagine all of us have taken solo endeavors that stand out in our memories.

> **PERSONAL TAKE:** Look back at Ruth 1:3-5. How might these past tragedies have weighed on Ruth as she carried out Naomi's plan?

Perhaps the same resolve that ushered Ruth to Bethlehem also carried her to the threshing floor that night.

Scripture doesn't reveal Ruth's inner conversation as she discreetly walked to the threshing floor. We don't need to take much of a leap to think how her heart must have been fluttering, what fears haunted her, how often she thought about turning back to Naomi's as Orpah had turned back to Moab. Had she misread Boaz's cues of kindness as meaning something they didn't? Would her heart be broken again? Would he reject her? And in the chance Boaz wanted her, could she risk the possibility of tragedy striking twice? I imagine the list of reasons for turning around mounted with every step, though perhaps the same resolve that ushered Ruth to Bethlehem also carried her to the threshing floor that night.

> **PERSONAL RESPONSE:** Describe a time when your obedience to God felt like a risk. What did you learn in the process?

Yesterday I mentioned we'd further explore the clothing Ruth wore to meet Boaz. You'll remember that the translation "best clothes" may not be the most accurate picture. The Hebrew word used to describe what Ruth wore, *śimlâ*, was a generic term. It normally referred to an outer garment that covered virtually the entire body except the head. Some commentators believe that Ruth dressed as a bride based on other extrabiblical passages that follow a similar pattern, but we can't know for sure what she wore. We do know that Ruth was dressed for a new day. She had changed her clothes.

By telling Ruth to change clothes, Daniel I. Block explains,

> It appears that Naomi is hereby advising Ruth to end her period of mourning over her widowhood and get on with normal life. . . . It may well be that until this time Ruth had always worn the garments of widowhood, even when she was working out in the field. Perhaps this was the reason for Boaz's inertia. As an upright man, he would not violate a woman's right to grieve the loss of her husband nor impose himself upon her until she was ready. We know too little about how long widows would customarily wear their mourning clothes, but it may be that Naomi is now telling Ruth the time has come to doff her "garments of widowhood."[5]

What striking imagery. Though many of us have not experienced the devastating tragedy of losing a spouse or someone we deeply love, we have known a time when God asked us to take off our mourning clothes, clinging, grasping, wishing, hoping, striving, and even praying for something and move forward. I specifically remember a moment when God made this exact request of me. I had been clinging to a past relationship, hanging on to the last ragged edges of something He had gone to great lengths to move me on from. Heavens, I had worked hard to move on from it. A passage in 1 Samuel 15–16 helped move me forward.

The story details King Saul's demise. God took the kingdom of Israel from Saul's hands because he'd failed to carry out God's commands. Saul's disobedience and the tearing away of the kingdom left the prophet Samuel in mourning for many years (15:35). Samuel had a vested interest in Saul's success since he was the one through whom God anointed Saul king over Israel. After a lengthy season of mourning, the Lord asked Samuel a penetrating question.

READ 1 SAMUEL 16:1. What was the question?

What did God then ask Samuel to do?

The Lord used this account to ask me how long I was going to mourn for the old because, indeed, He had something new for me ahead. It was time for me to move forward—without my mourning clothes. We keep our mourning clothes on when we daydream about the past, visit social media pages that remind us of the life we used to live, carry on conversations that tether us to the old way of doing things, and stop by previous stomping grounds that can easily transport us backward. When we're wrapped in garments of mourning over the past, we're unavailable for whatever else God has for us now. We sideline ourselves. Though we don't know exactly what Ruth had on, we know her new dress signaled a change, a readiness, an availability to Boaz and to God for the possibility of something new.

> Seasons of mourning, lament, and recovery are needed and right, and they look different for everyone and every new trial.

If you've experienced a devastating loss, I wouldn't dare presume on your grieving process. Seasons of mourning, lament, and recovery are needed and right, and they look different for everyone and every new trial. My hope is that when God has held us, healed us, and lifted our heads, we'll be ready to move forward with Him. While we may always bear certain losses and aches, we don't have to wear our mourning clothes while carrying them.

Isaiah 54 is an inspiring passage about God's love and faithfulness to the Israelites. Even though that passage focuses on a time when God redeemed the Israelites specifically from the consequences of their sin (a noticeable difference from Ruth's uprightness before God), I can't help but wonder if the author also had Ruth in mind when writing it.

READ ISAIAH 54:1-5. According to verse 4, what will be remembered no more?

Verse 4 doesn't say we won't remember our "widowhood," but the disgrace of it. We may always carry the painful memories, but God in His mercy is able to take the sting out of it. I well recall difficult times from my past, but they don't hurt like they used to. I praise God for the ways He binds up the brokenhearted.

PERSONAL REFLECTION: Do you sense that God is asking you to throw off some weighty garments? Old attachments, unforgiveness, bitterness, anger, despair, unhealthy habits, or anything else that might be keeping you in a stagnant place? Journal your thoughts.

PERSONAL RESPONSE: Will you hand those worn clothes over to Him in prayer? (Don't rush this if God is speaking.)

I've had a handful of experiences where God spoke to me through His Word as clearly as if I could hear His voice. I don't know how to describe it except to say these few experiences have been landmark moments for me. The passage I want to close with today constituted one of those moments. I was listening to a Bible teacher simply read this Scripture, and as she read it, the Holy Spirit spoke it over my life. It brought fresh meaning to the author of Hebrew's description that the Word of God is alive and active, sharper than a sword, penetrating the soul (Heb. 4:12).

FLIP BACK A FEW CHAPTERS AND READ ISAIAH 43:18-19.
What two things did God tell Israel not to do (v. 18)?

What did God promise was coming (v. 19)?

When we choose to dwell on old things, we stay in old places, even when God is doing a new thing. He's holding out a new dress for each of us. Isaiah 52:1a says, "Wake up, wake up; put on your strength, Zion! Put on your beautiful garments, Jerusalem, the holy city!" This is an Old Testament plea to the Israelites, but in Jesus Christ, we're called to the same awakening, the same new set of clothes. Do not dwell on the past! Yes, we all have our Moab stories, our past losses, aches, and stains; Christ has come that we might have new life (John 10:10).

READ EPHESIANS 4:22-24. How can you specifically put these verses into practice?

> Take off the old; put on the new. Be available to the living God.

Take off the old; put on the new. Be available to the living God. This may not mean a midnight visit to the threshing floor, but whatever the journey is for you, it all starts with the first step of obedience. "Therefore, if anyone is in Christ, he is a new creation; the old has passed away, and see, the new has come!" (2 Cor. 5:17).

DAY 3
LIE DOWN

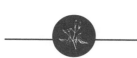

Nothing's quite so vulnerable as the first time you share your feelings in a relationship.

Nothing's quite so vulnerable as the first time you share your feelings in a relationship. I suppose the heart exposure wouldn't be so scary if only we could know how the other person would respond. Will our love be requited? What if the person isn't sure how he feels, rejects us, or, worst-case scenario, wants to just be friends? I confess I feel a little beyond all this anxiety. The online dating scene couldn't be any less suited for my personality, and I'm not in many settings where lots of single men are around. Unless for a direct intervention of God, I've settled into my life as a single woman, which may sound godly or terribly lazy. Still, Ruth's journey holds much that is dear to me. My prayer is that it will become dear to you, too, whether you're longing for a husband, a child, a better marriage, or deeper friendships. God knows the longings of your heart.

If proclaiming love for another person can be risky, Ruth's situation was in a category all its own. She had loved and lost before, was a lowly foreigner seeking a wealthy Israelite, a woman approaching a man (which was countercultural at best), and in a place she hadn't been invited. What more could she lay down in the middle of the threshing floor?

READ RUTH 3:5-9.

What kind of a mood was Boaz in after eating and drinking? Circle your answer.

Disgruntled   Pensive   Elated   In good spirits

How did Boaz come to find someone at his feet?

Yesterday you noted that Ruth carried out all that Naomi had asked of her (v. 6). I've been thinking about this recently in the context of mutual submission. As Christ-followers, one of the things we're called to is gracious deference to one another.

READ EPHESIANS 5:21 AND 1 PETER 5:5.

PERSONAL TAKE: How do you see Ruth displaying some of these New Testament characteristics to Naomi?

While Ruth did all that Naomi told her to do, she made an additional move. How did Ruth veer from Naomi's plan? (Compare Ruth 3:4 with 3:9.)

READ EZEKIEL 16:8 to further understand the action of a man spreading his skirt (the garment or covering referred to in Ruth 3:9) over a woman. In light of this verse, what do you think Ruth was asking of Boaz?

Threshing floors, Boaz sleeping in a skirt (more on this shortly), and Ruth asking him to spread his skirt (or wings) over her are unusual customs compared to the marriage proposals we're used to today. While taking a walk around one of my favorite nearby lakes, I passed a young man on one knee proposing to his girlfriend. I felt a little bad stumbling upon their engagement. Their friends were hiding behind trees capturing the whole thing on their phones, eyeing me like I should have checked with them before deciding to exercise that day. I can only imagine how awkward it would have been for a Bethlehemite who decided to go for a last-minute midnight stroll through the threshing floor.

Sometimes God calls us to add action to our prayers.

After following almost all of Naomi's instructions flawlessly, Ruth peeled off on her own. Instead of waiting for Boaz's instructions (3:4), she went for a marriage proposal. I love Ruth for this. She is brave, bold, humble, and thoroughly surprising. She didn't make this request out of single desperation or reckless nervousness. Many scholars suggest that Ruth was selflessly thinking of Naomi when she asked Boaz to marry her, knowing his redemption of her would also ensure Naomi's future security. The *hesed* Ruth demonstrated here is extraordinary.

The word *skirt* or *garment* can be translated as "wings," which you may see in your translation. Verse 9 could read, "Spread your wings over your handmaid." I love the use of the word *wings* here because it's reminiscent of an earlier conversation Ruth and Boaz had.

Look back at Ruth 2:12 and write out Boaz's prayer for Ruth.

In some ways, Ruth was asking Boaz to be the answer to his own prayer. Similarly, we remember when Naomi prayed that Ruth would find a husband, only for Naomi to later find out that God would use her to answer her own prayer for Ruth (1:9). There's something convicting here. Both Naomi and Boaz were the fulfillment of their own prayers for Ruth's life. We should never undermine the unparalleled power of prayer, and yet sometimes God calls us to add action to our prayers. Instead of uttering half-hearted prayers and moving on with our day, what would it look like if we intentionally prayed for others while looking for ways we can cooperate with God's redemption in their lives?

PERSONAL RESPONSE: What is something you've prayed a lot about but haven't been very active in? What can you do to change this?

LOOK BACK AT RUTH 3:7. Ruth approached quietly, uncovered his feet and _____ _____.

All of Ruth's anxieties, apprehensions, fears, wonderings, and emotions culminated with these two words. She had lost her husband, left her family, moved to a foreign country, inserted herself in the fields, submitted to her mother-in-law, journeyed to the threshing floor, and now, after all this time, she lay down. She had cast her life, her future, and even the legacy of her deceased husband at the feet of Boaz; there was nothing to do now but rest and wait.

Total surrender to God is one of the hardest places to reach but the most freeing place to arrive. Some of you have been working, toiling, and struggling—you've done all you can do and now it's time to cease striving and lie down at the feet of Jesus. I don't know what plagues you, what you're carrying, or what fears loom in your life, but I know you're not meant to carry them apart from Him. First Peter 5:7 is an encouragement to cast "all your cares on [Christ], because he cares about you."

Ruth could only bring herself to the threshing floor, make her request, and lie down. What imagery. As we think about what surrender looks like in our own lives, we'll look at a few verses that will help us find rest on our personal threshing floors. Instead of lying at the feet of Boaz and wondering what might happen, we will lie at the feet of Christ with full assurance that He knows us, holds us, and will only treat us with perfect love.

Read each verse slowly and thoughtfully as you envision getting to that place of rest. Note what is meaningful to you next to each reference.

Proverbs 3:5-6

Matthew 10:39

(continued on next page)

Matthew 11:28-30

Romans 12:1-2

We can't make a better choice in our lives than total surrender to Christ. It may be scary. It can be costly. But its reward is unparalleled. What Christ can do with a willing life surrendered at His feet is more than we can comprehend. Ruth couldn't have imagined what her story would turn into if given a thousand years to dream. I can assure you, we don't want to miss it for whatever we're clutching.

What Christ can do with a willing life surrendered at His feet is more than we can comprehend.

PERSONAL RESPONSE: What keeps you from resting under your Redeemer's wings?

Write your prayer of surrender here.

DAY 4
A CLOSER RELATIVE

Ruth was a seamless blend of confidence and humility, strength and deference, knowing what she wanted but knowing her position. It's hard to get this right without coming off as brash and arrogant or pitiful and self-deprecating. I believe it was Ruth's commitment to God that allowed her to strike this remarkable balance. "Unless God's inspiration had been in Ruth, she would not have said what she said or done what she did."[6] We may want to emulate her bravery and determination, yet it was the God of Israel who carried her to such heights. Her story reminds me of Psalm 18:35, which says that God stoops down to make us great. Yes, this story is about Ruth, but so much more about our God.

I hope you're up for a little twist today. Things are beginning to go almost too well, and this usually doesn't make for great storytelling. Not that the story was written for the sake of entertainment, but I will never miss an opportunity to grab the popcorn.

> **READ RUTH 3:10-13.** Boaz's first words to Ruth's request were, "May the LORD bless you" (v. 10). How would these opening words have reassured Ruth?

Ruth was a seamless blend of confidence and humility, strength and deference, knowing what she wanted but knowing her position.

"Given the spiritual climate in the period of the judges, an average Israelite might have welcomed the night visit of a woman, interpreting her presence as an offer of sexual favors, but not so Boaz."[7] Boaz's and Ruth's moral uprightness shine while so many others were doing only as they saw fit in their own eyes. Their actions encourage us to hold fast to the moral truths of Scripture, even the ones society mocks. (See Phil. 2:15.)

I suppose what is especially meaningful to me here is that God is able to work at any time, in any place, through anyone He chooses. This is not a standard scenario no matter how you slice it, and yet God is at work, fulfilling His redemptive agenda.

What did Boaz say that all the townspeople knew about Ruth (Ruth 3:11)?

What type of person did Ruth not go after for marriage, according to Boaz (v. 10)?

PERSONAL TAKE: What do you think Boaz meant when he said that Ruth's kindness (*ḥesed*) was greater than what she had shown earlier? (Look back at 2:11 to be reminded of her earlier *ḥesed*. Also, your previous answer might help you think through this question.)

Remember that the word *ḥesed* had to do with loyalty and devotion.[8] Ruth had shown great *ḥesed* to Naomi when she left her homeland behind. Now she was showing even greater *ḥesed* to Boaz by choosing him over the younger, possibly more attractive, men. But there's more to it than this. Because Ruth saw Boaz as a family redeemer, she also chose what was best for Naomi as well.[9] She put others before herself, casting her lot with the people of God and the family He placed her in.

This is not a prescriptive passage for us, meaning we aren't under obligation to marry for the benefit of our family members. Hallelujah. Not to mention, kinsman-redeemers aren't part of the culture we live in. But we can pull important and meaningful principles from Ruth's actions.

PERSONAL REFLECTION: What inspires you about Ruth's loyal devotion to Naomi and her family's legacy? How does her example of self-sacrifice inform your own decision-making?

Boaz referred to Ruth as a woman of noble character. I can't imagine what life would be like if we were judged by our character over our appearance. In my twenties, I made a personal declaration to myself that I was never going to be one of those people who worried about visible aging, and then FaceTime® and Zoom® happened at the same time I hit middle age. The creases, the meager eyelashes, the disappearing eyebrows—I'm worried about all of it! I have always wanted to be more beautiful than I feel I am. But at this point—now more than ever—I realize how fleeting it all is. I'm starting to believe deep in my heart, not just my brain, that the quality of a beautiful heart toward God really is more precious than gold, or glowing skin.

Prior to studying the book of Ruth, I didn't know that the Hebrew Bible places Proverbs right before Ruth, which means the description of the Proverbs 31 woman leads straight into Ruth's story. (Those of us who are unapologetic Bible nerds will find this thrilling.)

READ PROVERBS 31:10-31.

Don't get stressed about how perfect this woman appears or how we all feel like sloths compared to her. I feel confident this is not the aim of the chapter. Instead, focus on her remarkable constitution and strength. Notice what she values. Look for the areas you'd like God to bolster in your life. She's inspiring if we choose not to be annoyed.

PERSONAL RESPONSE: What things do you admire about her that you'd like to develop in your own life?

PERSONAL RESPONSE: List the things that remind you of Ruth.

Where does verse 31 say this woman will be praised?

> Now don't be afraid, my daughter. I will do for you whatever you say, since all the people in my town know that you are a woman of noble character.
>
> **RUTH 3:11**

Keeping this detail in mind, turn back to Ruth 3:11. Several translations say the "people in the city" or "fellow townsmen" knew Ruth was a woman of noble character, but the actual translation is, "all the gate of my people." It essentially means the same thing as all the people, but when the word *gate* is not included, we miss the significance.

Iain Duguid explains it this way, "The idiom is usually lost in translation, but what we see in Ruth [3:11] is precisely a 'Proverbs 31' woman in the flesh; her deeds have indeed been praised in the city gates!"[10] This is remarkable because the city gate was where important meetings and decisions happened.

We talked a little bit about this at the top of Session Four, but Ruth's fame is rooted in her character. It's not who she aligned herself with, whom she manipulated, her wealth, her beauty, her social following, her publicist; it's not about her heritage, her musical talent, or athletic prowess. It's about the *hesed* she has shown Naomi, Boaz, and Yahweh. And much like the woman in Proverbs 31:31, her renown and reward went all the way to the city gate.

PERSONAL RESPONSE: How does the celebration of Ruth's character encourage you to be faithful in the quiet and small, everyday things? (Matt. 6:18b and Luke 16:10 also speak of this principle.)

You've been so patient, dutifully reading about character and noble women and answering questions, but I know what you're thinking: *Who's this nearer kinsman-redeemer? We don't want him; we want Boaz!*

That there was a nearer kinsman-redeemer may explain why Boaz didn't propose to Ruth earlier and why she ultimately ended up on the threshing floor asking for an engagement. We can't be sure, but we do know this really throws a wrench in our story. If this unnamed relative chooses to redeem her, Boaz must step aside. Ruth takes this information in and then Boaz essentially tells her to sleep tight. I wonder if she slept at all. I would have been bug-eyed, staring up at the night sky, wondering what in heaven's name I had gotten myself into. Was Naomi's whole scheme God-inspired, or was she perfectly nuts?

What did Boaz promise to do if the nearer relative chose not to redeem Ruth?

I wonder how Ruth felt after hearing Boaz's favorable response to her request mixed with the news that someone else might want to redeem her. Nothing is ever easy, is it? It seems there always has to be a wrinkle of some sort. The lack of resolution and surprising turn in the story speaks to real-life circumstances, doesn't it? Most of life is not cut and dried, and yet we will see none of this surprises God, nor does it stop His will from being accomplished.

PERSONAL REFLECTION: The complicated nature of Boaz's response reminds us that nothing is too complicated for God to work out. Where do you need to apply this reassuring truth to your life today?

If Ruth slept at all that night she must have slipped imperceptibly in and out of reality, for who could possibly tell the difference between this and a dream? A Moabitess, a widow, poor with no standing, lay at the feet of a noble and powerful man who this time didn't just invite her for lunch or leave her extra sheaves but wanted her to be his wife. Ruth's dreams and reality were colliding. Boaz wanted to redeem her. Whether or not he could is a different story. But for the first time since arriving in Bethlehem, Ruth went to sleep knowing he wanted to.

DAY 5
A GIFT TO GIVE

What says provision more than a handful of grain?

My dad and brother are accomplished bread makers. They wouldn't claim this for themselves, but people who regularly feed their sourdough cultures like they're keeping a pet alive in the refrigerator should be considered experts. My dad makes two loaves nearly every day in part for nourishment but more for therapy. I finally joined the bandwagon and bought a stone mill that grinds wheat berries into flour. I'm a novice, but I love the breadmaking process and am slowly improving my skills. It is strangely satisfying to pour whole grain into the top of the mill and watch it land in my mixing bowl as fine flour. I also like the cathartic nature of kneading the dough. I enjoy shaping it for the loaf pan, watching it rise in the oven, and the aroma it casts through my house. My favorite part I suppose is eating it fresh out of the oven, though all the bread experts tell you not to slice your bread until it's cooled. These people clearly know nothing about happiness or butter.

All this talk of harvest fields and threshing floors and measures of grain has become a bit more meaningful to me since milling my own grain and making bread. What says provision more than a handful of grain? Grain will take center stage in today's reading, proving meaningful on both a physical and spiritual plane. You will love today's passage even if the closest you've ever gotten to a wheat berry was a loaf of Wonder Bread®.

READ RUTH 3:14-18.

PERSONAL TAKE: Why do you think Boaz didn't want anyone to know Ruth had come to the threshing floor?

What gift did Boaz give Ruth, and who was it for primarily?

Boaz didn't want Ruth going back to Naomi "_____ -handed" (v. 17).

LOOK BACK AT RUTH 1:21. In what condition did Naomi claim that the Lord had brought her back to Bethlehem?

The gift of grain was specifically for Naomi, although Ruth would surely benefit from Boaz's generosity. Boaz likely sent a gift to Naomi because it was part of fulfilling the biblical role of the *gō'ēl*. Remember that Boaz was a relative of Naomi's late husband, Elimelech (2:1), so his ultimate duty was to her.[11] In addition, the grain may have represented a down payment of sorts that assured Naomi either he or the other kinsman-redeemer would marry Ruth.[12] It may have been Boaz's way of telling Naomi, *I'm committed to taking care of this.*

> **PERSONAL REFLECTION:** Given this background, how did the gift of grain go beyond physical nourishment? In other words, what bigger provision did the grain represent?

The amount of grain Boaz loaded up in Ruth's shawl is difficult to determine because no specific measurement is given. It's safe to say it was a generous amount. I know we were all hoping that the weight of fear and anxiety Ruth lugged to the threshing floor would be replaced with an enormous bag of grain. Could she not have just one moment without gleaning, toting, or hauling? Does anyone know where the spa is in this town?

I do wonder how the weight of this grain felt on her back as she plodded back to Naomi's. Was it as feathers under her newly discovered knowledge of Boaz's affection, or did it drag like stones as her future still hung in the balance? I imagine that when Ruth made her way to the threshing floor the previous night, she figured that, good or bad, she would return with an answer. To think that after all she had been through things were still up in the air would have made me want to sling my shawl at someone.

What did Naomi tell Ruth to do in Ruth 3:18?

Boaz's assuring words to Ruth at the threshing floor and his gift of grain to Naomi revealed Boaz's intention to help Naomi and Ruth. But how this would all work out was less than clear, especially with the news of a kinsman-redeemer who was closer in line. So, they waited.

The stakes couldn't be higher for Naomi and Ruth. In a patriarchal society, without a family relative coming to their aid, there was no hope for Elimelech's family name to be carried on, the restoration of Naomi's land, or sustained provision within society. They weren't merely waiting for incidental changes to take place in their lives; they were waiting for redemption. And their hope rested upon Boaz.

> **PERSONAL REFLECTION:** What are you waiting for right now? And if you're waiting on another person, how can you place your expectation in God instead?

I don't know what you're waiting for right now. For me, I'm waiting for a house project to be finished so I can move back into the rest of my home and return to some semblance of order—porch furniture and mattresses in the living room isn't my ideal. But this is the small stuff. I'm also waiting on much bigger things to change in my world—some healing to take place, some relationships to be restored, some clarity of work direction. What I'm realizing, though, is I'm not so much waiting for circumstances to change as much as I'm waiting on the Lord to act, whatever that may look like. I'm also waiting on Him to change me.

I believe both Naomi and Ruth rested well because of their confidence in Boaz. Even though they weren't in control of the outcome or details, they trusted the heart and abilities of their family redeemer. How much more can we rest in Almighty God?

Read the passages below and answer the corresponding questions.

READ PSALM 27:14. What does waiting on the Lord cause our hearts to do?

READ PSALM 37:7. When we wait on the Lord, what do we no longer have to worry about?

READ PSALM 38:15. What reason does the psalmist give for waiting on the Lord?

READ ISAIAH 40:29-31. What did Isaiah say would happen to those who wait on the Lord?

In biblical terms, waiting does not mean inactivity, nor is it some resignation to fate. Naomi came up with quite a plan for Ruth. Ruth was faithful and loyal in following Naomi's plan, and she even took the extra step of proposing marriage. Boaz responded with a plan of action. But at some point, the word *wait* showed up as it always does (Ruth 3:18). Inevitably, there comes a moment where we've done all we can do, and the only thing left is to confidently rest in God's ability to handle the matter in His time and way.

Our God is worthy of our trust.

The passages we looked at today about waiting on the Lord are rooted in our confidence in Him. Just as Naomi and Ruth could trust that Boaz would accomplish redemption one way or another, so our God is worthy of our trust.

PERSONAL RESPONSE

Part One: In relation to what you're waiting on, is there anything the Lord has asked you to do that you haven't done yet? If, yes, write out your action step.

Part Two: If you've done all you know to do, write a prayer of confident trust in God's heart toward you and His power to accomplish His work in His time.

Before we close our week, I want to draw our attention to something we can practically emulate from today's passage. Even in the middle of Ruth's waiting, God was providing. Ruth received grain from Boaz and then carried it home to Naomi. She acted sacrificially from the beginning, committed to Naomi's well-being. Ruth was a remarkable force of fortitude and character, yet as a foreigner in an ancient society, she was still reliant on the kindness of Boaz. She could only give Naomi what she'd been given. This is true of us today. Jesus says in John's Gospel that apart from Him we can do nothing (15:5). Let's look at a New Testament story of this reality.

READ MATTHEW 14:13-21.

Whom did Jesus tell to feed the multitudes (v. 16)?

What was the disciples' response (v. 17)?

What was Jesus's response in return (v. 18)?

After Jesus blessed and broke the loaves, He gave them to the
_____ (v. 19), and they gave them to the
_____ (vv. 19-20).

Are you trying to give others what you don't have? Are you serving out of exhaustion, increasingly becoming frustrated or embittered along the way? When I feel this is happening, I try to reset. I pull away with the Lord, remembering that we were never meant to pour out of our own paltry resources. God has called us to be deliverers of His gifts, not the creators of them.

PERSONAL REFLECTION: Ruth receiving from Boaz and the disciples receiving from Jesus reminds us that we have nothing to give apart from our Redeemer. What area of your life does this speak truth into today?

God has called us to be deliverers of His gifts, not the creators of them.

PRAYER: Close in prayer. Put before the Lord your needs and the needs of those around you. Ask Him to meet them out of His abundance. It's my prayer that you will find yourself with even more than six measures of barley to carry home in your shawl.

WATCH

WATCH the Session Five video teaching and take notes below.

To access the
video teaching
sessions, use the
instructions in
the back of your
Bible study book.

CILANTRO CHICKEN ENCHILADAS

If you need comfort food, look no further. This has been one of my favorites for years. It feeds a crowd, makes great leftovers, and though it's rich, it's got some whole food gems like cilantro, cumin, and black beans. Your family and friends will love you for this one.

(SERVES 6–8)

INGREDIENTS

6 chicken breasts (boiled 20 minutes; keep 2 cups of broth)

2 cups of canned chicken broth

8 burrito size tortillas

8 tablespoons of picante sauce

½ cup of tightly packed cilantro

½ cup of sour cream

1 teaspoon of cumin (I use more)

1 tablespoon of flour

½ stick of butter

4 ounces of grated jack cheese

4 ounces of grated cheddar cheese

1 can of black beans, optional

DIRECTIONS

1. In a blender, combine cumin, cilantro, sour cream, 1 cup of canned chicken broth, and 1 cup of reserved chicken broth.

2. In a skillet or saucepan, heat butter slowly and add flour until smooth. Slowly add 2 remaining cups of chicken broth until smooth and creamy. (I usually add more flour to make it thicker.) Add to sauce in the blender. This is the "gravy."

3. To make enchiladas: Take each tortilla and fill with 1/3 cup of shredded chicken and 1–2 tablespoons of picante sauce. Add black beans if desired. Roll tortillas and place in a 9"x13" pan, seam side down. Fill the pan with gravy, completely covering the enchiladas. Sprinkle cheeses on top. Bake at 350° uncovered for 30 minutes.

Turn to pages 184–187 for appetizer, side, and dessert ideas that go well with this dish.

REDEMPTION

I took my first trip to the Amazon in the summer of 2009. I spent a week on JMI's wooden boat, *The Discovery*, learning the valuable life skill of sleeping through the night in a hammock. This is harder than you think when caimans (Brazil's alligator-like species) are clicking, frogs are groaning, and the occasional rooster, whose inner clock is nowhere near accurate, is crowing like its roost is on fire. Not to mention the shocking ranges of humidity. The upside is no one is paying for dewy skin over there.

It was a most memorable week. I swam in the Amazon. I caught my first piranha. I ate my first piranha. (This was before my friend told me she caught one with a leech crawling out of its eye, which abruptly ended the piranha portion of my Brazilian diet. Back to rice, beans, and twelve types of bananas.)

Every morning our schedule hung on a whiteboard. Tuesday evening's read: "Hunting Alligator." This ended up being a very friendly catch-and-release program, by the way, where the caimans got to get their pictures taken in the boat with Americans. I think they were really happy about this, as evidenced by how quickly they swam away to tell their friends and family about this honor.

At first, the caimans were proving quicker than our jungle guide Milton, so he decided to go with a different approach—a little number I like to call, "Diving on Top of Caimans at Midnight in the Amazon." Milton explained that caimans can't open their mouths underwater, which most of us found not relieving at all. Indeed, he came up with a catch this way, though for a moment we thought he'd been pulled in by an anaconda or that he'd jumped on the one exotic caiman in the Amazon that could open its mouth underwater.

Everyone in his own way was looking for opportunity to bring about redemption in another's life.

That first night on the water captured me for life. As did the jungle hikes where we saw monkeys and April accidentally stepped on a boa constrictor. I held a homemade torch and drank "milk" from a tree, and April wore a rain hat that our guide, Bjgode, made out of a leaf. It kept her drier than the forty-dollar rainproof hat she'd bought at DICK'S®. We drank pure, homemade acai juice, which is supposed to be the healthiest berry in the world and tastes like the healthiest berry in the world. It is only drinkable after fourteen teaspoons of sugar.

But more wonderful than the roosters, sky, scorpions, fish, shooting stars, coconuts, and hammocks were the people—beautiful and bright Christ-followers whose faith is boots-on-the-ground alive. They are patient, grateful, and content amidst their needs and sufferings. Their joy is truly from another kingdom. I remember my dad telling a group of indigenous jungle ministers, "Your work may not show up in the headlines. Your stories may not make *The New York Times* Best Sellers list. Presidents and kings may not know of you. But yours are the truly great stories. The ones written in the annals of heaven." And I believe it. Their understanding of what true greatness is aligns with Christ's definition—the greatest among you are the ones who serve (Matt. 23:11).

Although Boaz's and Ruth's stories have endured generations, I don't think either of them was thinking about what fortunes they might haul in for their efforts. Boaz wasn't looking to redeem Ruth for the humanitarian accolades, nor was Ruth sticking with Naomi for a reality show about living with your cantankerous mother-in-law. And to give Naomi credit where credit is due, she was loyal to Ruth despite what I imagine were many disapproving glances from Hebrew neighbors for having a Moabitess in her home. It seems that everyone in his own way was looking for opportunity to bring about redemption in another's life.

As we jump into this week, I wonder whom you might spread your wings over. Whom can you serve? Whom will you commit to love even if others find your commitment overly zealous or just plain foolish? Boaz reminds me that clutching our possessions and ease of life will always be at the expense of a wealth of Ruths and Naomis who not only need redemption but who might one day be redemptive in our own stories.

MAY THE LORD MAKE
THE WOMAN WHO
IS ENTERING YOUR
HOUSE LIKE RACHEL
AND LEAH, WHO
TOGETHER BUILT THE
HOUSE OF ISRAEL.

Ruth 4:11

DAY 1
I WILL; I WON'T

Let's continue our habit of rereading the chapter we just finished.

READ ALL OF RUTH 3. Note your fresh thoughts.

When it seems like nothing is happening, God is still working, perhaps most deeply on our faith.

Naomi's voice drew chapter 3 to a close: "My daughter, wait until you find out how things go, for he won't rest unless he resolves this today" (v. 18). Last week we pondered this theme of waiting, especially when a situation is out of our hands. I remember being on a boat in the Amazon with a dear ministry partner, John Paculabo. He said, "The people here know how to wait. They wait for clean water. They wait for food. They wait for the floods to recede." John was pointing to a fundamental part of their reality, one we're not as used to in our world of on-demand, hot and now, Instagram®. The people of the river assume that waiting is part of life and it isn't to be resented. The believers there, in particular, wait with hopeful endurance knowing the promises of Christ are both here and on their way.

I've learned from my fellow Brazilian brothers and sisters in Christ that those with immediate resources to solve any problem may be the ones most at a disadvantage. When we can fix things ourselves, we forgo the blessing of waiting and watching for the Lord to act in ways far beyond our abilities. And when it seems like nothing is happening, He is still working, perhaps most deeply on our faith.

READ RUTH 4:1-6. True/False. The name of the closer kinsman-redeemer is mentioned in the text.

What opportunity did Boaz present to him?

After agreeing to redeem the property, what made him suddenly change his mind?

Boaz went to the city gate because the gate was where business matters took place in ancient Judah. Though he knew the other kinsman-redeemer would eventually pass by, the way it's written highlights God's providential hand intersecting their paths. On the threshing floor, Boaz mentioned Yahweh's name to Ruth when speaking about her redemption (3:13), so it's reasonable to assume God was already intervening.

After Boaz invited this family relative to sit down, he included ten of the town's elders as witnesses, men who presided over judicial matters.[1] Our modern settings are far removed from these customs, but "these verses represent an ancient equivalent to modern transcripts of court proceedings."[2] What Boaz wanted to accomplish was an important legal matter.

If you had difficulty finding the other family relative's name, you're where the narrator wants you. Boaz called him *peloni almoni*, two rhyming Hebrew words that would be like our rhyming phrases *helter-skelter* or *hocus-pocus*. Our closest translation is probably something like "so and so."[3] Perhaps Boaz didn't want to be too friendly with his competition. When Boaz initially brought to the attention of Elimelech's relative the idea of redemption, he didn't mention Ruth; he only mentioned property. Once again, land in the Old Testament was to remain with one's family if at all possible (Lev. 25:25-30). The succession went from sons to daughters to the closest male relative.

It appears that buying the property appealed to this other male relative. He didn't even have to think about it before agreeing to redeem. But Boaz left out an incidental detail—marrying the Moabite widow. This sort of shows a sly side to Boaz, which I appreciate. It's a move that reminds me of one of my favorite quotes from Anne of Green Gables: "Well, I wouldn't marry anyone who was really wicked, but I think I'd like it if he could be wicked and wouldn't."[4] Though we've seen no wickedness in Boaz, it's nice to know he can unfurl his tricky side when he must.

How did Boaz refer to Ruth in Ruth 4:5?

PERSONAL TAKE: Why do you think the caveat of acquiring Ruth was a deal breaker for the nearer kinsman? Look closely at verse 6 and give it some thought.

Iain Duguid says this about the problematic transaction, "If there were to be a child from the relationship with Ruth, the redeemer would lose the field and there would be no benefit to his own children and estate to compensate for the costs involved in taking care of Naomi and Ruth."[5] So it wasn't just a marriage to Ruth that threw the deal out for this relative. Perhaps the even greater problem was that if Ruth were to bear a child, an heir of Elimelech's, the child would inherit the land this redeemer would have worked so hard to purchase and maintain. And that's not all—he would have helped to keep Elimelech's line alive, something he was more interested in doing for his own family and legacy.

Although we studied the multifaceted role of kinsman-redeemer (*gō'ēl*) in Session Four, Day Five, I want to remind you that marriage was not part of the required duties. Remember that we also looked that day at another custom in Israelite law called Levirate marriage that may have played into Boaz's proposal to the closer relative.

LOOK ONCE AGAIN AT DEUTERONOMY 25:5-10. What appears to be the purpose of Levirate marriage?

The idea of Levirate marriage would have been familiar to Boaz and the closer relative, but since neither of them was Elimelech's immediate brother, marriage to Ruth was not binding on either of them. As mentioned before, the role of a kinsman-redeemer didn't require marriage to the person being redeemed. This makes Boaz's proposition to the *gō'ēl*, which included marriage to Ruth, unique. The *gō'ēl* could have legally purchased the land but passed on Ruth. But considering that Boaz put forth the moral obligation to redeem Ruth, the *gō'ēl* probably didn't feel comfortable doing less than that. Boaz was after the spirit of what a kinsman-redeemer represented, not merely the letter of its execution. Boaz wanted to marry Ruth, something the closer relative was not prepared to do.

What has been puzzling for scholars is that Boaz took on a role that was not exactly characteristic of the kinsman-redeemer's duties nor did his proposal fit Levirate marriage. This is a detail that means a lot to me as someone who would sometimes rather do my "spiritual duty" than serve as far as love will

The role of a kinsman-redeemer didn't require marriage to the person being redeemed.

carry me. Self-sacrificial love isn't confined to rule books or formulas. It's not interested in checking boxes but in fulfilling the spirit of God's heart toward His people.

We probably can't fault "so and so" too much for refusing to redeem any more than we can fault Orpah for heading back to Moab after Naomi's urging her to return. He was simply making a logical business decision while looking out for his own family and inheritance. Adding Ruth to the deal wasn't profitable or beneficial for him or his descendants, so he simply passed it up. What's significant to me is not what he did wrong but what Boaz did extraordinarily right. The decision of the *gō'ēl* not to redeem was reasonable, but when I study Scripture, I see that *reasonable* is not what usually goes down in history.

> **PERSONAL RESPONSE:** What sacrificial, scary, risky, or costly decision have you made in obedience to God? And what were the results? (Be honest if it hasn't been easy.)

I wonder if your life can be easily explained. If most of your decisions are simply based on what benefits you and your life, I encourage you to note the difference between Boaz and the unnamed *gō'ēl*. One did the extraordinary and the other the expected. One chose sacrifice and love while the other chose safety. One left a legacy in the pages of Scripture; the other was never heard from again.

> **PERSONAL RESPONSE:** If the Lord is calling you to do the unusual, illogical, or sacrificial, write about it below. And if you long to live such a life, let the Lord know you are willing.

The *gō'ēl* did what seemed best for him, much like Orpah did what was best for her, but neither are ever heard from again. Ruth, Boaz, and Naomi share a legacy we are still celebrating today.

One of my friends left her well-paying, established position at a great company to become the executive director at JMI. It meant a big pay cut and an uncharted path. So uncharted that boat rides down the Amazon River and treks through the Moldovan countryside would be part of her new normal. I watched her wrestle this decision out with the Lord. I knew she was going to get there with Him because it was so obvious He was asking her to do this. It was only a matter of time for her to see it too. She took the job with JMI, and there are not enough words to describe all that God has done in just eight years. She wouldn't have missed it for what was safe and predictable. Another one of our friends told her, "I don't want you to look back and think, *I wonder what God would have done if I'd obeyed*. I want you to look back and say, 'Look what God did.'"

DAY 2
TO BE WILLING

One of the most important things we can do while reading the Old Testament is to look for Jesus in the story line. When Jesus approached the disciples after His resurrection on the road to Emmaus, He showed them how their ancient Scriptures had been speaking about Him all along, beginning with Moses and the prophets (Luke 24:27). I haven't wanted to draw every possible line between Boaz and Christ because comparisons can be overdone. I have also wanted to stay in the context of Ruth as much as possible so we can further acquaint ourselves with the laws and customs of the Old Testament. But today, as we consider three characteristics of a kinsman-redeemer, we won't be able to help running to our New Testaments, finding Christ as our perfect and all-sufficient Redeemer.

One of the most important things we can do while reading the Old Testament is to look for Jesus in the story line.

REREAD RUTH 4:1-6 TO REFRESH YOUR MEMORY.

Today we'll focus on three important characteristics of a kinsman-redeemer. He was required to be:

1. Near of kin;

2. Able to redeem;

3. Willing to redeem.

> Which of these three kept the "so and so" relative from redeeming?

The nearer kinsman-redeemer was a family relative. He was able to redeem, but he wasn't willing. And isn't it this third consideration that often ends up being our downfall? This may be one of the most tragic ways for a Christian to spend her life: in the right place with all the right resources but without a willing heart. One commentator put it this way, "It remains . . . an instructive fact that he who was so anxious for the preservation of his own inheritance, is now not even known by name."[6]

PERSONAL REFLECTION: The obscurity of the nameless kinsman-redeemer, and what he missed out on, should inspire us to be willing to do whatever Jesus asks of us. What does that look like for you in this season of life?

Before we move on to some theologically profound points in today's study, I want to linger on this important aspect of Boaz's character—his sacrificial willingness. This, after all, is what set him apart from the other relative. Boaz made his decisions based on God's heart and the needs of others. I don't want to get to the end of my life and find I've missed having an eternal impact because I chose only what benefited me.

HOLD YOUR PLACE IN RUTH AND READ PHILIPPIANS 2:1-8.
Compare Paul's words to the Philippians with the qualities and actions we've seen in both Boaz and Ruth. What specific similarities do you notice?

Whose mindset or attitude did Paul encourage us to have (v. 5)?

PERSONAL REFLECTION: Is there an area of your life where you're unwilling? It might be an unwillingness to have the mindset of Christ, to be obedient, to help someone who is in need. If so, take some time to write about the tension you're feeling.

When I was a child, one of my favorite friends of my parents was Sherry Meddings, a zealous, full-throttle personality who happened to be a Bible teacher. She was also very into fashion and helping you discover what color palette looked best on you. When my closest friend at the time was on her way out the door to high school, Sherry said, "Don't think I'm too tired to notice you're in all black; you're not a 'winter' on the palette."

We lost Sherry to cancer when I was a teenager. I have no doubt I'd be at her doorstep this very moment if given the opportunity to laugh with her once again, to grapple with our strong-willed natures in light of God's merciful kindness.

One of her sayings was, "God can change your heart; you just have to be willing to be made willing." This always spoke to me when I wasn't in a state of willingness because if I could just be willing to be made willing, then the Lord would take care of the rest. I can't read about Boaz's willingness to sacrificially redeem Ruth and Naomi and Elimelech's land without thinking of Sherry.

> **PERSONAL RESPONSE:** If you are willing to be obedient to the Lord—or are willing to be made willing—write a prayer of surrender below.

Romans 12:1 says, "Therefore, brothers and sisters, in view of the mercies of God, I urge you to present your bodies as a living sacrifice, holy and pleasing to God; this is your true worship." I used to be afraid of dedicating my life to the Lord, certain He would seize this small window of opportunity to make my life extraordinarily hard or send me down the Amazon in a hammock (wait . . .). But I'm more convinced than ever that the most frightful and sad condition is in not yielding our lives to the Lord. He is our hope, our joy, our peace, our strength, our abundant life. There is no adventure like the willing life.

It's now time for us to trace the idea of kinsman-redeemer into the New Testament. When I think of Ruth and Naomi, their impoverished positions, and their vulnerability as they most likely waited at home for Boaz to act, I'm reminded of our own powerless state apart from Christ. We were unable to redeem ourselves from the curse of the law, powerless to save ourselves.

> **READ ROMANS 5:1-8.** How does verse 6 speak to this truth?

We need a Savior who fulfills all three qualities of a kinsman-redeemer. From memory, write the three qualifications.

Look up the following references and draw a line matching each verse with its corresponding quality.

Mark 10:45   Christ was near of kin (became like us).

Hebrews 2:14-15   Christ was willing to redeem.

Hebrews 7:24-25   Christ was able to redeem.

In our powerless, hopeless, sinful state, we were given a Redeemer, a Redeemer who left heaven and was made like one of us in human flesh because we needed a Savior who was near of kin. But we needed more than someone related to us. We needed someone who is able to redeem us, and only One qualified for the task. Because we were bound by the curse of the law, we needed someone who was perfect and therefore stood outside the law. And so God gave us a Redeemer who was able. As we saw yesterday in the character of the closer relative, we would be hopelessly stranded if our redeemer were near of kin and able but unwilling. And here is where Jesus Christ perfectly fulfills the role of kinsman-redeemer. He was not only close and able, but He was also lovingly willing to redeem.

PERSONAL RESPONSE: What does Christ's willingness to save you mean to you?

Jesus Christ was not only close and able, but He was also lovingly willing to redeem.

Therefore, there is now no condemnation for those in Christ Jesus, because the law of the Spirit of life in Christ Jesus has set you free from the law of sin and death. For what the law could not do since it was weakened by the flesh, God did. He condemned sin in the flesh by sending his own Son in the likeness of sinful flesh as a sin offering, in order that the law's requirement would be fulfilled in us who do not walk according to the flesh but according to the Spirit.

ROMANS 8:1-4

DAY 3
A NAME

I was out in the middle of Lake Sunapee on a wooden Donzi speedboat when I first heard the phrase *midlife crisis*. I wasn't more than eleven or twelve at the time. "Dad," I asked, "what's a midlife crisis?"

What does my name mean to people? What will it mean when I'm gone?

"Well," he explained, "it's when people get to be a certain age, usually somewhere in their forties, and they start questioning the meaning of life, and they try to discover who they are by buying things and chasing experiences."

I was perplexed. Why would you not know who you are by the time you're as ancient as forty? And how would getting new things help you figure that out? I was positively lost. Fast forward all these years later and I'm not chasing new toys or new relationships, and I'm not having an existential crisis, but I at least get the sentiment. There's a certain reckoning in your mid-forties when you consider what your contribution to this world is, and for Christians, your contribution as a Christ follower. I've thought more in the last few years about the legacy I want to leave as a believer in Christ than I've thought about it my whole life. *What does my name mean to people? What will it mean when I'm gone?*

Today we'll come across more ancient customs, one having to do with people taking off their sandals and giving them away, as well as some other interesting legal proceedings. But mostly we're going to focus on the importance of a name in a way that's less about fame and more about redemption and preservation. It's a relief when we're not the ones having to preserve and promote our own names, not to mention a whole lot more biblical. I'm looking forward to exploring this with you, midlife crisis or not.

READ RUTH 4:7-10. What did taking off a sandal and giving it to the other person symbolize in ancient Israel?

What additional family names are mentioned in verse 9, differing from verse 3?

Verse 10 says that Boaz "acquired Ruth the Moabitess." What is one of the reasons given for why he did this?

We just read the legal proceedings that allowed Boaz to purchase Elimelech's property and marry Ruth.* The property purchase and marriage would take place later, but today he was officially recognized as not just *a* kinsman-redeemer but *the* kinsman-redeemer now that the other *gō'ēl* had relinquished his right to redeem. We also discovered that in addition to Boaz having the rights to Elimelech's property, he was taking on whatever belonged to Chilion (Orpah's late husband) and Mahlon (Ruth's late husband). Redemption was abounding, spilling over the edges of reason. Even those who had been buried in the dark land of Moab were being resurrected in name and legacy through Boaz's goodness and sacrifice.

But it is Ruth who takes center stage at this point in the story. She was the primary treasure Boaz was after. We've been waiting a long time for this moment, ever since Ruth and Boaz first stumbled upon each other in the middle of a field. Yahweh is even better than any of us could have imagined Him to be. The name of the once destitute Moabitess widow was ringing out through the city gates as Boaz proudly said in the presence of witnesses that he was taking Ruth, the Moabitess, Mahlon's widow, to be his wife! She was far more important to him than the estate he was gaining.[7] Listen to what Daniel I. Block says about Boaz's proclamation, "The use of the full name . . . may be required by the legal context, but it is evident that *Ruth's Moabite status is no barrier for Boaz*" (emphasis mine).[8] Do we not love this with all our hearts?

Ruth's Moabite heritage might have been a deal-breaker for the other *gō'ēl*, but it was no issue for Boaz. He was unashamed of who she was and proud to acknowledge whom he was marrying before the elders and the townspeople at the city gate. This is one of those occasions when we can take our ink pens and draw a line from Boaz to Christ. The God of Israel has always been about the poor, foreigner, fatherless, and widow. It is from this God that Boaz learned to be a loving, selfless redeemer. But Boaz would not be the ultimate expression of God's heart for the nation of Israel and beyond. This expression would come through the incarnation of our Lord, Jesus Christ. The One who is still calling us by name.

Note: For historical accuracy, Naomi was not technically selling her property. As a widow, she did not own Elimelech's land. Rather, this exercise allowed Boaz the legal right to Elimelech's property, per Naomi's presumed consent.

READ ISAIAH 43:1. How did God call His people Israel?

READ JOHN 10:1-3. How does Jesus, our Shepherd, call His sheep?

READ JOHN 20:10-18. At what point did Mary finally recognize Jesus after His resurrection?

I grew up in a church tradition that passed the communion elements through the aisle on Communion Sunday. We were corporately addressed by the pastor, but we weren't individually served. I don't regret the way we partook of communion, and I appreciate the various traditions. In recent years, though, I've been in churches and settings where the person administering the elements will offer them to me and say, "Kelly, this is Christ's body broken for you. This is Christ's blood poured out for you." I can't make it through without tears. It's the sound of my name in connection with Christ's broken body and spilled blood. It's the sound of your name. The law, weakened by our human nature (Rom. 8:3), is an incapable savior. Jesus takes the law's sandal, fulfills the law Himself, redeems us by name, and then declares, "You are all witnesses!"

> **PERSONAL RESPONSE:** We all have a name, a history, and a wake of good and bad. How does Boaz's proclamation of Ruth's name and history as he vowed to redeem her help you better understand what Christ has done for you? Do you believe He delights to take all of you?

In keeping with this theme of names, you noted earlier that one reason Boaz married Ruth was out of a selfless act to preserve Elimelech's name and property (or inheritance). If no one chose to redeem, Elimelech's name would have forever disappeared from his property and from history, one of the worst things that could happen to an Israelite. Instead, by purchasing Elimelech's land and marrying Ruth, Boaz selflessly kept

Elimelech's name alive and connected with his property. As well, Boaz and Ruth's first child would carry on the legacy of the family.[9] This is a stunning act of *ḥeseḏ* on Boaz's part, a posture of heart we're to have in even greater measure as followers of Christ. We also see that in sacrificing his life to preserve Elimelech's name, it was actually Boaz's name that has been preserved through history for countless generations.

Our names have worth and meaning because Christ redeemed us for Himself.

PERSONAL RESPONSE: What is one way you can continue to seek the good and longevity of someone in your life? This may be for a parent, child, spouse, friend, or coworker. Give this some thought.

I started today by writing about my own desire to have impact and a name that matters. What's superior to making a name for ourselves is having Christ call us by name. Better than finding our way to the tables of the who's who is being invited to the wedding feast of the Lamb. Our names have worth and meaning because Christ redeemed us for Himself. We may think we have to cover our pasts or insecurities or heritage or Moabitess-ness, but as Boaz called Ruth by her full name, so Christ called us by ours.

PERSONAL RESPONSE: What meant the most to you in today's study? Write your response here.

DAY 4
A BLESSING

I can't say that the two verses we're going to read today are two of my very favorites because I've said this too many times in too many of my Bible studies. If you have too many favorites it begins to water down the meaning of the word *favorite*. People stop listening to you. So, I will begin by saying that today's reading is much beloved, a choice selection of Scripture, preferred by me on any given day, like a cluster of fruit in season. What do you think?

I love a spoken blessing. We probably don't speak enough blessings over one another.

Ruth 4:11-12 records a collection of blessings spoken by the surrounding witnesses in response to Boaz's declaration to marry Ruth (v. 10). I love a spoken blessing. We probably don't speak enough blessings over one another. There's way too much talk these days of sending good energy and vibes and thoughts. These are fruitless sentiments. As we will see today, the community surrounding Ruth and Boaz did not merely send kind thoughts; rather, they spoke God's blessing. They pointed to His faithful acts in the past as a way of preparing Boaz and Ruth for what He might do for them and all of Israel in the future. Every word was based not on their positive energy but on God's immutable character.

READ RUTH 4:11-12. Let's examine the witnesses' blessing in sections. Fill out the following:

What two women did the witnesses want Ruth to be like? What had these women helped do (v. 11)?	
What did the witnesses want for Boaz in both Bethlehem and Ephrathah (v. 11)?	
Whose house did they want Boaz's house to be like (v. 12)?	

When the crowd said "we are witnesses," this legally affirmed agreement.[10] To understand this unique series of blessings, we need to research the Old Testament names mentioned. For ancient Israelites, Rachel, Leah, Tamar, Judah, and even Perez were household names like Oprah, Tom Brady, Michael Jordan, and Princess Diana.

HOLD YOUR PLACE IN RUTH AND LET'S BEGIN BY READING ABOUT RACHEL AND LEAH IN GENESIS 29:16–30:24. Fill in this family tree using the verses you just read.

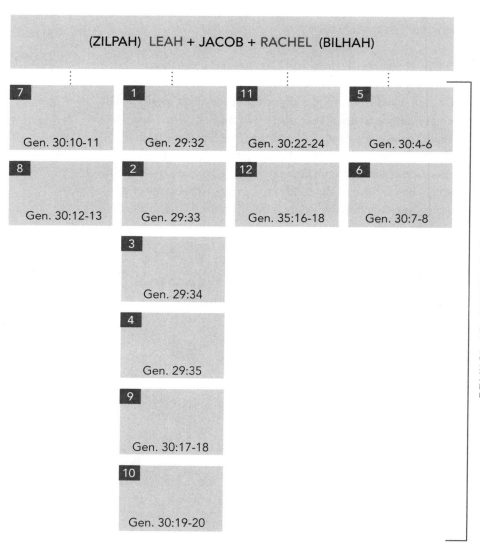

(ZILPAH) LEAH + JACOB + RACHEL (BILHAH)

| 7 | 1 | 11 | 5 |
| Gen. 30:10-11 | Gen. 29:32 | Gen. 30:22-24 | Gen. 30:4-6 |

| 8 | 2 | 12 | 6 |
| Gen. 30:12-13 | Gen. 29:33 | Gen. 35:16-18 | Gen. 30:7-8 |

3
Gen. 29:34

4
Gen. 29:35

9
Gen. 30:17-18

10
Gen. 30:19-20

TWELVE TRIBES OF ISRAEL

PERSONAL REFLECTION: Rachel and Leah were considered the matriarchs of Israel. How does this deepen the significance of what the witnesses wanted for Ruth?

Genesis 49:1-27 gives an account of twelve of Rachel and Leah's (and their maidservants') children concluding with, "These are the tribes of Israel, twelve in all" (v. 28). When we look at this history, we begin to understand how unprecedented and astounding the witnesses' blessing was over Ruth. They were calling for a widowed, childless Moabitess to be blessed with the kind of fertility given to Rachel and Leah who had multiple and distinguished children, ones who built up the house of Israel. Not only was the community embracing Ruth as a true Israelite, they were looking for her to play a prominent role in their society and legacy. As Robert Hubbard states, "Having achieved equality with Naomi (4:3), she was no longer a Moabite, foreigner, or girl, but *wife*."[11] God delights in using us, no matter our culture or histories.

> God delights in using us, no matter our culture or histories.

PERSONAL RESPONSE: How does the witnesses' blessing on Ruth affect the way you see God's ability to redeem your past? Or, is there anyone in your life you've given up on seeing God redeem? How can this passage inform your prayers for yourself and others?

Let's look at a few more people to fully appreciate the blessing of the elders and the townspeople. We touched on the significance of Judah in Session Three, Day Three. He was the father of the tribe of Judah from which both Elimelech and Boaz descended. Judah had a son named Perez by a woman named Tamar.

READ ABOUT JUDAH, TAMAR, AND HER SON PEREZ IN GENESIS 38:6-30.

What did you learn about Perez, and what was unique about his birth (vv. 27-30)?

Since Tamar had been widowed before having children, the witnesses may have been highlighting her as the inspiration for how God could also bless Ruth with a child who could impact Israel's future. What might be more significant is that Tamar was a foreigner and yet she became the mother of Judah's most prominent clan. Consider Hubbard's notes on verse 12: "The author probably implied two theological points about Yahweh in that theme. First, Yahweh cared as much for all the world's Ruths—i.e., all its outcast foreigners—as Boaz did for Ruth. Second, God actually desired to 'redeem' them into fellowship with himself. In sum, the theme voiced earlier reaches its climax here: Yahweh welcomes foreigners who demonstrate the faithfulness demanded of ethnic Israel."[12] Ruth shared with Tamar the seeming hopelessness of being an outsider without a husband to carry on a family line. If God could pull Tamar into His plan of redemption, could He not also use Ruth?

In summary, the people of Bethlehem wanted Ruth to be like Rachel and Leah because their children built up the house of Israel. They wanted Boaz's line to be like that of Perez who was born to Judah and Tamar because this was the clan Boaz descended from and the most prominent of Judah's sons in Israel's history.[13]

Tracing these Old Testament names and wading through ancient customs is not easy, and you've done great today. Well done. As we close, I want to touch on a portion of the blessing that goes along with yesterday's study on the preservation of someone's name. Ruth 4:12 finds the witnesses blessing Boaz with standing and fame in Bethlehem. How ironic that Boaz's decision to preserve someone else's name (Elimelech's) turned into his own fame and recognition. His sacrificial redemption of Naomi and Ruth proved to make a lasting name for him forever embedded in the Scriptures. Perhaps this is just a little of what it means in Luke 9:24 when Jesus said, "For whoever wants to save his life will lose it, but whoever loses his life because of me will save it."

You may be laying your life down for your children or your husband. Perhaps you're about to get married and enter an altogether new level of self-sacrifice. Or maybe you're single and you're giving your life to friendships, family, and ministries. Maybe you've been asked to take care of your parents, or you've taken in a family member, or you've adopted a child. No matter your situation, laying down your life for others, for the sake of Jesus, is never wasted. No matter how quiet, how humble, how thankless, God is making a name for you— one that is dear to His heart.

LOOK BACK AT RUTH 4:11. Who would ultimately be responsible for Ruth and Boaz bearing a child who would help build the house of Israel?

Verse 11 reminds me that Boaz, Ruth, and Naomi could all do their parts, but without God Almighty it was futile. Sometimes I've erred on the side of thinking that if I obey God or sacrifice for someone else, then God owes me. (He does not, by the way.) At other times, I've been lazy and slipped into thinking that it doesn't matter what I do because God is going to do whatever He wants anyway. Ruth, Naomi, Boaz, and the witnesses' recollection of Old Testament history remind us that God's people are called to God-like action—sacrifice, kindness, hard work, generosity, inclusion of outsiders, other-centeredness, all of which can be summed up in the word *ḥeseḏ*. At the same time, God's miraculous work of redemption belongs to Him. He alone can achieve it. This is why throughout the book of Ruth we see people saying, "May the LORD" do such and such. What happens is ultimately up to Him, but in His goodness, He invites us to participate with Him while living with hope and expectation in His promises.

Laying down your life for others, for the sake of Jesus, is never wasted.

DAY 5
A WEDDING, A BABY

Boaz took Ruth and she became his wife. He slept with her, and the LORD granted conception to her, and she gave birth to a son.

RUTH 4:13

Up to this point I have really loved the narrator of Ruth. The author has done some nifty things with pacing, word selection, and phrasing. With an economy of words we've been given a compelling story that has transcended centuries and cultures. But I have a point of contention. How is it that after all this time, a marriage, a pregnancy, and a birth have been squeezed into a single verse? Could we not linger a moment? Shall we not tarry amidst the details? I don't think it would have been too indulgent for each of these life-altering events to at least have its very own verse. In a story where we've been given details like how many pounds of barley Ruth could carry, I don't think it would have been too over the top to know what kind of dress she wore or the flavor of her wedding cake. The good news is that we can saunter through this verse at our own pace, savoring each delicious event.

Fill in the blank: "Boaz took Ruth and she became his _____" (v. 13).

PERSONAL REFLECTION: What do you think of this news? Does it surprise you? Does it make you hopeful?

Ruth had gone from foreigner to maidservant to maiden to wife.[14] God drastically changed Ruth's life. Like all stories with roots and foundations, this didn't happen overnight. Each stage gave way to the next almost imperceptibly, which is what steady obedience and God's faithfulness often look like. What an inspiration to keep going knowing that God will give the increase.

I wrote my first Bible study about modern-day idols and called it *No Other Gods*. One of the main characteristics of serving false gods is that we must constantly downgrade our expectations of them. We start with high hopes and dreams that a certain idol will deliver happiness, excitement, and well-being to our lives; but because a false god is false by its very nature, our expectations must continually be lowered until we're in total bondage to something that doesn't even resemble anything close to what we had originally hoped. But not so with the one true God. With Him we find the opposite. The more we get to know Him and the more we trust and serve Him, the more our expectations ascend and our realities bloom.

PERSONAL RESPONSE: Ruth was described as the Moabitess, the foreigner, and the woman beneath the servant girls. Now she was a celebrated wife and a true Israelite. How has God changed your life? What has He brought you from? (Don't skip this because it takes thought and heart. Spend time reflecting.)

What is the Lord credited with in verse 13?

This is an important mention and only the second time the Lord is shown directly intervening in the book of Ruth.

Look back at 1:6b. What was the first instance?

God was directly involved in this moment. It's not that He hadn't been present or working throughout the story, but since we know that Ruth was married to Mahlon for ten years and without children, Ruth 4:13 implies her pregnancy was a divine act of the Lord.

Several references in Scripture show God's hand in conception. Look up the references and name the corresponding woman next to each verse.

Genesis 29:31

Genesis 30:22

1 Samuel 1:19-20

Luke 1:24-25

PERSONAL TAKE: Out of all the opportunities for the narrator to have inserted God's direct hand, why do you think the narrator chose to do it in reference to Ruth's conception?

We've looked at Ruth's marriage and pregnancy, and now I want to close by looking at the significant birth of her son, whose name had not yet been revealed. He would not only be a blessing to Ruth and Boaz, but we'll find out next week that this child would be a surprising gift to Naomi. Further still, he took his place in a line that would permanently bless the nation of Israel.

LOOK BACK AT RUTH 1:11-13. What was Naomi's biggest reason for persuading Ruth and Orpah to return to Moab?

We just can't conceive of what God has in store.

This is good medicine for those of us who can only think of one way for a particular situation to be resolved. I get stuck all the time in the quicksand of my narrow perspective. Naomi saw herself as the only way to procure another husband for Ruth, and therefore a son. She was too old, so she wrote the whole thing off. It never occurred to Naomi that Ruth would bear her own Israelite child who would one day be Naomi's redeemer. We just can't conceive of what God has in store. This lifts my head when I'm discouraged and can't understand my own way.

READ RUTH 2:11-12. Now that we're further into the story, list all the ways Yahweh answered Boaz's prayer by repaying Ruth for all she had done.

Ruth had given birth to a son. She had lost, she had loved, and now she was leaving a legacy. This son would save Elimelech's name from being forever lost. He would preserve Naomi's legacy, which had been hanging by a thread since her husband and sons died in Moab's faraway land. He would give Boaz a great name and fulfill the blessing the elders and witnesses spoke over him—that he would have great standing and fame throughout Bethlehem. He would help preserve Ruth's own name as one who, indeed, helped build up the house of Israel. And this is just the beginning.

Next session we will look at the incomprehensible reaches of Ruth's legacy, a blessing that has extended to this very day and no doubt will extend into eternity. Let us not forget that it all began with a woman who left her home to live in the land of the God under whose wings she had come to take refuge. I imagine every true legacy begins this way.

> **PRAYER:** This week we've talked about stepping out in faith, being willing (or willing to be made willing), believing that we can trust God with our future and that He knows our full name. Close with a prayer over the one thing that touched you most this week.

WATCH

WATCH the Session Six video teaching and take notes below.

To access the video teaching sessions, use the instructions in the back of your Bible study book.

SOUTHWEST CHICKEN SOUP

*My friends and I make this several times during the fall. In my
mind, it's synonymous with chips and salsa, autumn leaves,
and football season. What makes this special is the salsa verde.*
(SERVES 6)

INGREDIENTS

12 oz. of jarred salsa verde (or make your own!)

3 cups of cooked chicken (You can use an oven-roasted chicken from your grocery to save time, or you can use a recipe for a whole chicken.)

15 oz. of cannellini beans, drained

3 cups of chicken broth (You can use canned broth for a soupier mixture.)

1 teaspoon of ground cumin (I use more!)

1 package of frozen corn

Chili powder to taste

2 green onions, chopped

Sour cream

Tortilla chips

DIRECTIONS

1. Empty salsa into a large saucepan. Heat 2 minutes over medium-high heat. Then add chicken, beans, broth, cumin, corn, and chili powder. Bring to a boil; lower heat to simmer for 10 minutes, stirring occasionally.

2. Top each serving with onions, sour cream, and chips.

Turn to pages 184–187 for
appetizer, side, and dessert
ideas that go well with this dish.

LEGACY

I always knew the day would come, but I was no less surprised when it actually happened. I was driving to a rehearsal on a Saturday morning when my mom called to tell me my grandfather on my dad's side passed away. It would be only a few short weeks later, on the same day of the week, that I'd get the same news about my grandmother. And just a few months later, my dad would call saying my other grandfather, affectionately known as Pop, had left us too.

It was a lot of loss in a short amount of time. Both sets of grandparents loved us deeply and brought us into their worlds. My Grandpa Minter and my Pop Cowen were both successful in their careers. Grandpa was a retired admiral in the Navy and former superintendent of the Naval Academy. He fought in three wars, was skipper of the Intrepid, and gave President Kennedy a tour of the Academy shortly before he was assassinated. My Pop ran several Sears® and Roebucks® in Brazil. When he and his family returned to the U.S., he bought a struggling flower shop and turned it into a booming florist in Boca Raton.

Personality-wise, the two of them couldn't have been more different. Grandpa was loving and warm toward us grandkids, but he was a towering, accomplished military man. Pop was a prankster who would do things like plant fake salamanders in the shower when we'd come to visit. At my sister Katie's rehearsal dinner, I sat across from Grandpa Minter, who was in his late eighties. He told me he'd been reading through the Bible and compiling a list of every question he had so he could take them before his minister. While my grandfather was in mid-sentence, I noticed out of the corner of my eye Pop blowing bubbles across the room with one of the party favors. That one instance captured them both perfectly.

> By the grace of Christ, you have a legacy to leave, and now is the time to invest in your legacy by investing in others.

All four of my grandparents left a profound legacy for us grandchildren. And the thing about receiving someone's legacy is you do nothing to earn it. I had precisely zero influence on the people who came before me or the examples they set. What my grandparents gave me by sharing their lives with me was a pure gift. The other interesting thing about legacy is although we can't control the ones we're given, we have every bit of influence over the legacies we leave.

This week we're wrapping our study on the book of Ruth, but we'll discover that this story doesn't really wrap. Because, legacy. The book ends with a genealogy that runs all the way to Christ and beyond. Not only is a physical legacy left but also a spiritual one that continues to produce in ways not confined to lineage. My dear friend, by the grace of Christ, you have a legacy to leave, and now is the time to invest in your legacy by investing in others. If it wasn't too late for an aged Hebrew landowner, or a childless Moabitess, or a destitute widow, it is certainly not too late for you and me.

THEY NAMED HIM OBED. HE WAS THE FATHER OF JESSE, THE FATHER OF DAVID.

Ruth 4:17

DAY 1
NAOMI

An otherwise humdrum list of names is actually the making of redemption's greatest story.

There's a quality about the close of something that can be both sad and rewarding. This is my ambivalence as we embark on our last week of study. Yes, it will be nice to recapture my life from the realms of Bethlehem and barley where I've lived for the past several months. But I will miss waking up thinking about you and how the story is shaping your heart. As we begin this final week, I hope you feel great accomplishment. You've given yourself to studying one of the most remarkable women in Scripture while, more importantly, opening your heart up to her God. (And if you've made any of the recipes, you've so overachieved.)

As you've probably noticed, the book of Ruth's remaining verses are dwindling, and the story line is drawing to a close. There's only one more recipe to try or destroy your kitchen with, depending on your culinary outlook. And if you're anything like one of my friends who first went through this study with me, you peeked ahead and noticed that we have mostly genealogies left which diminished your desire to finish. Fortunately, some of the most interesting parts of our study remain to be pulled out of that genealogical hat. Once we've done a little exploring, we'll see that an otherwise humdrum list of names is actually the making of redemption's greatest story. I'm convinced you're going to love it.

READ RUTH 4:14-15. Who suddenly took center stage?

After last week's notable events of Ruth and Boaz's marriage, pregnancy, and birth of a son, I wasn't expecting verse 14 to turn back to Naomi. I anticipated her character would slip backstage while Ruth and Boaz came out for a final bow. Instead, the narrator does the opposite. Ruth and Boaz exit the book's final scene while the spotlight falls somewhat surprisingly on Naomi and the new child. The book both begins and ends with her.

PERSONAL TAKE: Why do you think Naomi gets such significant billing here at the end of the story?

Who were the people who spoke to Naomi in verses 14-15?

You might remember "the women" from Ruth 1:19-20. Look back at these verses and note how Naomi responded to them upon her return.

I kind of like that no specific names are given, just "the women." Because we know who they are—if you grew up in church, they were the thick-as-thieves church ladies who were there when we were born, performed ridiculous skits at our church retreats, helped us celebrate our birthdays, wrote us generous checks for graduation, and cried at our weddings (or are crying because we haven't had a wedding yet). They're the ones who still come scrambling down the church aisle to give us a hug when we visit home. And to find out if we've met someone—and when exactly the wedding will be. They are *the women*. I don't know what else to say about it.

In Naomi's case, they were the ones who, in response to her return, threw the whole town into a happy uproar. Only women have this superpower. They were also the ones Naomi felt comfortable enough to tell, "By the way, don't call me Naomi. Call me a bitter old woman because God has made my life miserable!" You can only be this honest with your women. The same women who wept when Naomi left Bethlehem, rejoiced when she returned, and most certainly gossiped about her after she flipped out are now gathered around her at the birth of her grandson, speaking words of blessing over her. I would have liked to have been there for this, frankly, because church women know how to speak a blessing. It's in their bones.

THE WOMEN'S BLESSING IS RICH, SO LET'S LOOK CLOSELY AT RUTH 4:14-15.

Why is it significant the women blessed the Lord instead of Boaz?

What did they declare that the Lord had not left Naomi without?

The witnesses declared that Boaz's name would be famous in Bethlehem (v. 11), but how far did the women see this child's fame extending? Circle your answer.

To the Gentiles   Throughout Moab

Throughout Ephrathah   Throughout Israel

What two things did the women see that this child would do for Naomi (v. 15)?

Fill in the blank: Ruth _____ Naomi. And she was worth more to Naomi than _____ sons.

PERSONAL REFLECTION: If you were Naomi, which part of the women's blessing would have meant the most to you and why?

That Ruth carries the book's title and no doubt shines as the central character makes it natural to assume the story will end with her. Seeing that it doesn't, we have to assume this wasn't an arbitrary or accidental decision on the author's part but rather the divine inspiration for its conclusion. So, let's revisit some defining stages of Naomi's life.

Next to each reference, write down a few words that describe Naomi and her situation. (I filled in some for you as examples.)

1:1-2   Naomi moved to Moab because of a famine in Bethlehem.

1:3

1:4-5

1:6

1:11   Naomi urged her daughters-in-law to return to their homes.

1:20-21

2:18

3:1-4   Naomi schemed to get Ruth and Boaz together.

3:18

4:9

PERSONAL TAKE: After reminding ourselves of these details, what does Ruth 4:14-15 reveal about God's heart toward the sufferer?

PERSONAL REFLECTION: Let's personalize this. It's one thing to believe something about God's heart for other people, but how does God's gracious redemption of Naomi affect the way you view His heart in your current circumstances?

The intentional focus on Naomi at the close of the story is not what most of us expect. Linear thinking would say it's one thing for Ruth's life to be restored and celebrated because we all get the sense she deserved it. But it's another thing to see God's lavish blessing poured out on Naomi because she appears the less worthy character. No matter how much we say we believe in grace, we still like things to follow a certain pattern: The good sacrificial servant girl should get top billing in the final scene, and the sometimes ornery mother-in-law shouldn't get to hog the baby and the spotlight. Grace stuns our theories and carefully constructed notions of how things should go. It blesses those who don't deserve it, redeems names that would otherwise have disappeared, and sets glory in the bosoms of once-forsaken widows.

PERSONAL RESPONSE: Are you a linear thinker when it comes to grace? In other words, is your posture toward others one of kindness only if they deserve or earn it?

PERSONAL RESPONSE: And what about your relationship with God? Are you always trying to earn His favor, or are you a humble receiver of His undeserved mercy and grace?

Yahweh is the true Hero of the story, and unmerited favor is His specialty.

The story could easily have ended with its exceptional stars, Ruth and Boaz. But I believe the curtain closing on Naomi, encircled by a rejoicing community, holding a grandson she never imagined, while resting in a secured future was divinely deliberate. Yes, Yahweh rewarded Ruth and Boaz for their extraordinary obedience, but He also blessed and redeemed a woman who had lived in a land far from Him and who returned in deep bitterness. And she's the one the story ends with! Why? Because Yahweh is the true Hero of the story, and unmerited favor is His specialty. While we were still sinners, Christ died for us (Rom. 5:8).

I suppose the surprising ending of Ruth is good news for all of us. I can at least speak for myself that I am much more of a Naomi than I've ever been a Ruth. I'm grateful to see this lovely story leave its crown upon Naomi's gray head. It's just like God to do that.

PERSONAL RESPONSE: Close today's study by meditating on Psalm 103:8-18, thanking God for His grace.

DAY 2
A KING IS COMING

I may have inadvertently misled you yesterday when talking about the book of Ruth ending with Naomi. It ends with her more than it ends with Boaz or Ruth, but the *end* end is made up of a genealogy. And that genealogy will point more to God and ultimately to Christ than any of the story's characters. I clarify this because as much as we all can't get enough of a good love story or a rags-to-riches plot or a winning heroine or even a grace-filled turnaround of events for the somewhat undeserving, I don't think this book is specifically about any of those things. They are all wonderful aspects of the narrative, and even more so because each one describes what actually happened! But the meaning of the book—at least I think—is that God is about redeeming this broken world to Himself and nothing can thwart His grand plan of redemption.

Nothing can thwart God's grand plan of redemption.

When I first wrote this study, I was single and without children. As I write this updated version nearly twelve years later, I am still single and without children. I've made some crazy journeys in my lifetime (hello there, Amazon jungle), but I've yet to find a husband at the local threshing floor. The women have not laid a child in my lap, although my brother and his wife and three children now live around the corner from me, and this has been a redemptive development in my life that was totally unexpected. My point is that if we're looking for God to perform the exact miracles He did in Ruth, we may be disappointed. He has not promised to do for us what He did for Naomi, Ruth, or Boaz, though He may. What He has promised is to give us the Redeemer to which the book of Ruth points—Jesus. Let's continue looking to Him this week.

> **PRAYER:** As we move through these final days, you may be longing for a spouse, a child, a provision, a legacy, or something of similar importance. Share with the Lord the longings of your heart. Trust Him to provide in His time. And ask to experience more of Him because the Blesser always exceeds His blessings.

READ RUTH 4:16-17. We're finally told the name of Ruth's son. What is it?

You may be asking yourself why this group of women was naming Ruth's son. Interestingly, this is the only example in the Old Testament where someone other than the child's parents is recorded naming the child. Some scholars argue that the women were merely affirming the name that Ruth, Boaz, or Naomi had already given him.[1] Regardless, this scene is one-of-a-kind in the Old Testament.

Ruth 4:16 notes that Naomi took the child in her lap (or against her breast) and cared for him. We're not certain exactly what role was given to her, but it appears Ruth allowed Naomi to be a significant figure in raising Obed, perhaps something similar to a foster mother or nanny.[2] Though not a legal move, Ruth's great affection for, and not obligation to, Naomi allowed her an intimate place in caring for Obed.[3]

PERSONAL TAKE: Look back at verse 15. How is Ruth's affection for Naomi described? And how does this clearly play into Ruth giving Naomi a coveted role in Obed's life?

Granting Naomi this close-knit bond with her only son is another act of *hesed* on Ruth's part. Ruth is nothing if not made of self-sacrifice and kindness.

READ PROVERBS 11:24-25. How have you seen this proverb at work in each person's life?

Naomi

Boaz

Ruth

It seems that no matter how much Boaz and Ruth keep giving of themselves, they're no match for God's ability to give to them. This is not karma; it's not the universe equaling itself out eventually. This is not *If I do this, God owes me that.* It's a principle of God's nature.

He Himself is unyielding in His sacrificial love for us, and He delights in blessing those whose hearts are turned outward toward others as is His.

Ruth's unselfishness with her child (along with women such as Hannah, Elizabeth, and Mary) stands out against many Old Testament stories of prominent women often characterized by bitter fighting and jealousy around the ability to bear and raise children. We get the sense that it blessed Ruth to see the once hopeless Naomi rocking the child against her breast as if he were her own. This goes against our tendency to clutch and protect what's most valuable to us instead of blessing others with the gifts God has given us.

> **PERSONAL RESPONSE:** If you have children, is entrusting them to the Lord difficult for you? If you don't have children, what is another relationship you have a hard time entrusting to God? Why?

The meaning of Obed's name is not explained in the text. This is unusual when compared to other Old Testament naming practices. We know that Obed is an abbreviated version of Obadiah, meaning "servant of Yahweh." Obed is more ambiguous, simply meaning "to serve" or "one who serves."[4]

> How does the meaning of Obed's name seem to fit with the women's description of him in the first part of verse 15?

The surrounding context seems to tell us that Obed was given his name because he would serve Naomi by restoring her life, taking care of her in her old age, and keeping alive her family's legacy. As I mentioned earlier, in-between the first writing of this study and the revised version, my brother's family moved to Nashville. David and his wife Megen came with their two children, Will and Harper, and shortly after, Megen became pregnant with her third. I like to say I got Lily from scratch because she was the first of my nieces and nephews to be born in Tennessee. I have had her from day one.

From the perspective of an American aunt, as opposed to a Hebrew foster grandmother, I totally get this idea of children as renewing agents. I don't know how they do it, but my spirits are lifted when I'm around them. The phrase "renew your life" in verse 15 literally means "to cause life to return."[5] And as far as being sustained in my old age, I am really counting on at least one of them letting me live next door.

Though there's nothing else written about Obed in the Bible, we know he revived Naomi's heart from loss and hopelessness. He made the one who was once empty full again. We also know something else about him, something that made him a hugely significant player in the biblical narrative.

> Fill in the blanks using the CSB translation: "He was the father of
> _____, the father of _____" (v. 17).

The book of Ruth has had many surprising twists and bends in its four short chapters, but this may be the most stunning bit of news yet. The narrator reveals that Obed would be the grandfather of King David. In a few words the story has gone from being a quaint romance in the small town of Bethlehem to a national plot of redemption. And this is just the beginning. This surprise revelation affirms that the women's blessing was more prescient than any of them could have imagined.

> **REREAD VERSE 14.** How do we see the women's blessing of Obed now fulfilled?

We'll dig into the ramifications of this revelation later this week, but mull over one thing as you go: Remember this bit of information was implemented into the story many years after Ruth's death. When Ruth gave birth to Obed, she had no idea that a ruddy little shepherd boy named David was on his way. She knew nothing about an unparalleled intellectual named Solomon, or any other descendants for that matter. What she knew was that faithful obedience and love to God during her earthly years would affect things long after she was gone, even if she never got to see how.

> These all died in faith, not having received the promises, but having seen them afar off, and were persuaded of them, and embraced them, and confessed that they were strangers and pilgrims on the earth.
> **HEBREWS 11:13 (KJV)**

PERSONAL RESPONSE: Spend time speaking to God and listening to Him about your own legacy.

DAY 3
THE HEART

Today we'll look at the genealogy that ends the story. Each name is like a flower springing up in the garden bed of Perez. Who could have imagined all that God would do with the wayward Judah and his bereft daughter-in-law, Tamar? They had no idea of the names or families that would come after them—nor can we know our own legacies. Our duty is only to be faithful to God and let Him author the story.

> **READ RUTH 4:18-22.** The list begins with Perez. Briefly write what you already know about Perez, being sure to include who his father was. (Go back to Session Six, Day Four if you need a reminder.)

We know little about Hezron and Ram and not a great deal about Amminadab except that he was the father-in-law of the significant high priest, Aaron (Ex. 6:23). His son, Nahshon, was a major leader of the tribe of Judah, and his son, Salmon, about whom not much is known, was the father of Boaz. Of course, we know Boaz was the father of Obed, and, as we saw yesterday, the son of Obed was Jesse, and the son of Jesse was David.

> **READ 1 SAMUEL 16:1.** Where was Jesse from?

I grew up mostly learning Scripture compartmentally: Adam and Eve in the garden, Noah and the ark, Daniel and the lion's den, Mary and Joseph in the stable, Paul on the road to Damascus. I'm thankful to have learned these stories, sometimes several times over along the way, but seeing their place in the greater whole of Scripture is something I wish I'd been taught in more depth. This is why I get excited about the book of Ruth ending with a genealogy—because it ties Ruth, Boaz, and Naomi's smaller stories into a much greater one. It reminds us that our own stories too are part of God's divine narrative.

The book of Ruth ends with a genealogy because it ties Ruth, Boaz, and Naomi's smaller stories into a much greater one. It reminds us that our own stories too are part of God's divine narrative.

I wanted you to see that Samuel was sent to Jesse of Bethlehem because that immediately ties us back to how the book of Ruth began: "A man left Bethlehem in Judah with his wife and two sons to stay in the territory of Moab for a while" (1:1). It reminds us that generations before Jesse the Bethlehemite was born, his great-great-grandparents (Elimelech and Naomi) ventured off to Moab and almost didn't make it back. If it weren't for God intervening and ending the famine, perhaps Naomi never would have returned. And if it weren't for Ruth's determination to follow Naomi to Bethlehem, she never would have met Boaz. And had not Naomi sent Ruth to the threshing floor . . . you get the idea. The point is that a whole lot of unlikely things happened before we get "Jesse of Bethlehem."

> Let us draw near with a true heart in full assurance of faith, with our hearts sprinkled clean from an evil conscience and our bodies washed in pure water.
>
> **HEBREWS 10:22**

WITH JESSE'S HERITAGE IN MIND, KEEP READING 1 SAMUEL 16:2-13.

Which son did Samuel hastily think was the Lord's anointed, and why does Scripture suggest he thought so (vv. 6-7)?

Write out God's response to Samuel in verse 7.

Samuel, one of the godliest men of his day, made the mistake of judging by outward appearances. Samuel thought he knew what a king looked like—height, stature, a royal physique. But the Lord knew that the true measure of a king could only be determined from the inside. Only God had those eyes to see.

PERSONAL RESPONSE: In what areas do you fall into the mindset of judging by outward appearances (even if it's judging yourself)?

Our western culture doesn't help us with this. I realize that physical beauty is not a novel prize of our society. But it sits atop our value list. I'm going to guess that how we look is a multibillion-dollar industry. I have a new friend helping me with some work around my house, and she's just gorgeous, all the time, even when she's not trying to be. I feel saggy-skinned and worn around her, and she's done nothing to make me feel this way except being a naturally beautiful person. I can be too aware of what I do or do not look like. I want to think far more about what I offer people of Christ, what _hesed_ I can give them. I'm all for taking care of ourselves and being as physically attractive as is reasonable, but our lives and legacies are about far more. Even Ruth didn't run after the younger (read, more attractive) men.

> **PERSONAL RESPONSE:** Whose character and heart do you appreciate, and how has he or she blessed you? (This person may also be the most physically attractive person you know—inner and outer beauty aren't mutually exclusive, but only one truly matters.)

The heart is what builds legacies, and the Bible speaks a lot about it.

> Hold your place in 1 Samuel. Read the following verses and answer the corresponding questions:
>
> **READ DEUTERONOMY 8:2.** How and why did God test the hearts of the Israelites?
>
> **READ PROVERBS 4:23.** What are we to do with our hearts?
>
> **READ HEBREWS 10:22.** Because of Jesus, how does God allow us to draw near to Him?

TURN BACK TO 1 SAMUEL 16. Whom did the Lord tell Samuel to anoint, and where did his family have to go to retrieve him?

I see similarities between David and his great-grandmother, Ruth. David was brought from a humble field, and Ruth was gathered from a foreign land. Both were unlikely choices to carry on the royal line of Judah, and both needed someone greater and more powerful than themselves to see them—not just to see their outward appeal but the goodness of their character and purity of their hearts. This kind of seeing takes special vision.

TURN BACK TO RUTH AND READ 2:11 AND 3:11. Just as the Lord chose David because of his heart, why was Boaz drawn to Ruth?

First Samuel 16:12 says that David had beautiful eyes and a healthy, handsome appearance. He was an attractive man who may have had Boaz's smile, Ruth's eyes, or Naomi's coloring. But no matter what distinct features hung on through the generations, we know that both Ruth and David drew the eyes of the Lord.

> For the eyes of the LORD roam throughout the earth to show himself strong for those who are wholeheartedly devoted to him.
>
> **2 CHRONICLES 16:9a**

PERSONAL RESPONSE: Today's study is so personal that I don't want to specifically direct you. Close by responding to God however you feel moved.

DAY 4
RAHAB

In the Old Testament, legacy was measured by a person's physical offspring, in particular, the number of sons who could carry on the family name. In the New Testament, legacy is measured differently. Though marriage and childbearing are some of God's most precious gifts to us, they are not the only way to leave a legacy. As followers of Jesus today, the spiritual legacies we leave are the most significant. As we continue to look at Ruth and Boaz's genealogy, I want to remind you that even if you don't have children, you have an eternal legacy to leave as a child of God.

As followers of Jesus today, the spiritual legacies we leave are the most significant.

BEFORE WE RETURN TO THE BOOK OF RUTH, READ MATTHEW 12:46-50. How did Jesus define His family in this passage?

READ 1 TIMOTHY 1:1-3. How did Paul refer to Timothy?

READ GALATIANS 4:4-7. Paul said that because of Jesus we're no longer slaves but sons. And if we're sons, what does this also mean we are?

Remember, sons were the ones who carried on the family name and gained the inheritance in Hebrew culture. We've seen the ramifications of this firsthand in the book of Ruth. So, while it may at first seem offensive that Paul called both men and women sons, he was actually elevating the status of women. In a patriarchal culture, Paul showed that both men and women have the same spiritual standing as God's heirs.

I wanted to begin with these New Testament passages as a reminder of the spiritual legacy we're called to live as children of God. I'm also thinking of those who may have children or grandchildren who don't claim to be followers of Christ. This does not exclude you from leaving an eternal legacy through the impact you have on those around you.

PERSONAL RESPONSE: Think of a person who is not related to you but who has impacted your life. How has he or she done this?

Countless men and women who have never had children have impacted future generations in unparalleled ways. The central ingredients to leaving a divine legacy are loving God with our whole hearts, loving others, and teaching those around us to do the same.

We're finally ready to turn our attention back to the book of Ruth, but we're going to do this by reading Matthew 1:2-6.

The genealogy found in Ruth is included in these verses. Starting in verse 3, compare Matthew's genealogy with Ruth's (4:18-22). What three additional names did Matthew give besides Zerah?

It was not Jewish custom to mention women in genealogies, especially in royal ones. This is why we don't see any women in the book of Ruth's genealogy. It's no small thing that Matthew, a Jew, chose to include women in his genealogy. The significance is easy to miss in our modern western world where a woman can run for president or sit on the Supreme Court. In Jewish culture, these were bold insertions. We've researched Tamar, and of course, we know a lot about Ruth now, but today we want to see how Rahab fits into our story. Boaz has been too important of a character for us to not meet his mother.* We need important questions answered like, *What were her beliefs? Her strengths? Did she cook with a lot of barley?* We can find some of this out in the book of Joshua.

READ JOSHUA 2. For historical context, Israel's leader Joshua had sent spies into the land of Canaan to explore it before the Israelites attacked and entered the promised land.

How is Rahab described in verse 1?

Note: Salmon and Rahab may have been Boaz's grandparents, great-grandparents, or even further removed. Biblical genealogies often skipped generations, though we don't know this is the case here. Regardless, it seems Boaz would have been very familiar with Rahab and her story since family history was vital to the Hebrew people.

What did Rahab do to help the Israelite spies?

What signal did Rahab have to give to be spared by the Israelites when they attacked Canaan (vv. 17-18)?

What conclusion about Israel's God had Rahab come to (v. 11)?

PERSONAL TAKE: How did Rahab's belief about Israel's God change the course of her life?

PERSONAL REFLECTION: What impacts you the most about Rahab's story in light of her being the mother (or ancestor) of Boaz?

READ JOSHUA 6:15-17,22-25. Who were the people Rahab permanently made her home among? How is this similar to Ruth's story in Ruth 1:15-17?

The mother of Boaz was an outsider, a foreigner—the stuff we're used to with Ruth. But Rahab's work as a prostitute, chosen or forced upon her, placed her further outside the fringes of acceptable Israelite society than even Ruth. From far beyond those edges, God's love gathered Rahab and settled her among His people. There she would find a husband named Salmon and bear a son named Boaz who would one day be heralded as the great-grandfather of King David. This is the stuff of gospel groundwork, paving the way for the once and future King of kings.

For all whose pasts are sullied, who are sure they have nothing to offer, who don't feel worthy to find their place among God's people, I hope you will see the goodness of God at work in

Rahab. For the woman who's afraid her life cannot be spared, that she's only as good as her body, that it's too late to undo the damage, God's redemptive work in Rahab's life is but a flicker signaling the radiant light of Christ in whom condemnation cannot be found (Rom. 8:1). But we'll get there tomorrow.

PERSONAL RESPONSE: How does Rahab's story of coming to live among God's people speak to your own story? Be specific.

God's redemptive work in Rahab's life is but a flicker signaling the radiant light of Christ in whom condemnation cannot be found.

IN CLOSING, READ HEBREWS 11:31. What did the writer of Hebrews say Rahab did by faith?

PERSONAL TAKE: How do you think Rahab's story influenced Boaz's compassion for Ruth? This is a big question that deserves some thought.

PERSONAL RESPONSE: Spend time praying that God would give you a heart for the outsider. Ask Him to convict you of your prejudices and help you look at the heart.

DAY 5
A SAVIOR IS BORN

What an honor to write about a Moabitess who loved the God of Israel, who packed up her belongings to take care of a woman who wasn't blood and who didn't want her, who risked her life in the fields, who risked her life on the threshing floor, who drew the eyes of a noble man, married him, bore a son, and then placed the baby on the breast of the mother-in-law she so desperately loved. Ruth. It will forever be my privilege to have written about her.

The last name and the very last word of the book of Ruth is *David.*

And then there is the other great privilege of sharing this journey with you—getting to add my thoughts and passions to the pages of Scripture you've so purposefully studied. I only wish I got to hear more of your own insights, how Naomi, Ruth, Boaz, and God have changed your life, what you discussed with one another in your living rooms, churches, or favorite cafés over coffee and tea, perhaps with restless children running around. What recipes were your favorites, what moments of prayer the most penetrating. And if anyone decided that entrusting her life to God was infinitely worth it after all. Thank you. Thank you for this honor.

READ RUTH 4:22.

The last name and the very last word of the book of Ruth is *David.* We all know him as King David, Israel's most renowned and beloved king. His life is a study all its own. In short, God pulled him from shepherding flocks and anointed him as king over Israel. He was the pinnacle of Old Testament history, the most successful and dynamic king Israel ever had, and one of the most important characters in the Old Testament. To this day Israel's flag honors him with the Star of David as its central image.[6] I'm going to guess neither Ruth nor Boaz saw that coming. Even more important than King David's fame in Israel's history is the Ruler who would come after him. The Old Testament Scriptures foretold that Israel's promised Messiah would arise from King David's family.

READ 2 SAMUEL 7:12-16.

For context, the prophet Nathan was speaking God's words to David about his son Solomon building a temple for the Lord. But he also spoke to David about the future of his kingdom.

For how long would David's kingdom be established (vv. 13,16)?

READ ISAIAH 11:1-5,10. From whose "stump" would Israel's Messiah shoot?

READ MICAH 5:2-5. From what city would this great Ruler of Israel come?

READ ISAIAH 9:6-7, one of the most famous passages foretelling the birth of the Messiah. On whose throne would He sit?

Yesterday we read beginning in verse 2 of Matthew 1, but today I want to start at the top.

READ MATTHEW 1:1-16. According to verse 1, whose genealogy is this a record of, and who is announced in verse 16?

PERSONAL TAKE: Turn back to Ruth and read 1:11-14. How does Ruth's place in the line of Christ make the verses you just read even more significant?

I can't begin to comprehend God's sovereignty. What would have happened if Ruth had followed Orpah back to Moab? What if she hadn't been quite as determined to make the God of Israel her God? What if she gave into Naomi's reasoning—*she's right, I'll never find a husband in Bethlehem.* I don't know how Obed would have been born, or Jesse, or David, or Joseph, or what this would have done to the line from which Jesus came. I can't solve this mystery; all I know is that I'm glad Ruth didn't turn back, that she stayed the course. Her example inspires me to do the same.

PERSONAL RESPONSE: How does Ruth's unwavering commitment to God—and the astounding ramifications—encourage you to remain faithful in difficult times?

I presume we can't know how the biggest, as well as the seemingly insignificant decisions, affect our lives and those around us. It's a reminder of how important daily surrender is to the Lord. When our lives are His, when we trust Him to lead us, we can rest assured He will guide our steps and intersect our lives with the opportunities and people He lovingly and sovereignly purposes.

PERSONAL RESPONSE: As you ponder the past six weeks, what is the single most impactful moment you had during this study?

I'm amazed at how God masterfully preserved the line of Judah so many times over by the fragile threads of foreigners like Ruth, heartbroken widows like Naomi, affairs like Tamar's, prostitutes like Rahab, seduced women like Bathsheba, and humble teenagers like Mary. Only the gospel can make sense of such things.

> I hope you will leave this study with a fuller, deeper, and more supreme grasp of the good news of the gospel— the *hesed* of Jesus Christ.

If there is anything I hope you will leave this study with, it is a fuller, deeper, and more supreme grasp of the good news of the gospel: the *hesed* of Jesus Christ given to us. Boaz beautifully demonstrated it to Ruth, Ruth lavishly bestowed it upon Naomi, and even Naomi grew in *hesed* for Ruth. From all of these imperfect and unlikely intertwining relationships came a Son, a Savior, from the town of David, who would take away the sins of the world.

PERSONAL RESPONSE: Reflect on the following verses and close with a prayer of thanksgiving for our magnificent redemption.

"He has raised up a horn of salvation for us in the house of his servant David" (Luke 1:69).

"Today in the city of David a Savior was born for you, who is the Messiah, the Lord" (Luke 2:11).

"The shepherds said to one another, 'Let's go straight to Bethlehem and see what has happened, which the Lord has made known to us'" (Luke 2:15b).

"For my eyes have seen your salvation. You have prepared it in the presence of all peoples—a light for revelation to the Gentiles and glory to your people Israel" (Luke 2:30-32).

"This book and this genealogy demonstrate that in the dark days of the judges the chosen line is preserved not by heroic exploits by deliverers or kings but by the good hand of God, who rewards good people with a fulness beyond all imagination."[7] The book of Ruth ended with the name of King David. Ours will end with the name that is above all names, Jesus Christ.

WATCH

WATCH the Session Seven video teaching and take notes below.

To access the
video teaching
sessions, use the
instructions in
the back of your
Bible study book.

FRESH TOMATO PASTA

This is one of my favorite seasonal dishes to make. You really can only have this in summer when the tomatoes are in season because this is all about fresh tomatoes. Combined with fresh garlic, olives, feta, and pasta—I just gave you the whole recipe— you can't beat it. (SERVES 6)

INGREDIENTS

1 (12 oz.) package of dried linguine

4 large tomatoes, chopped

5 cloves garlic, minced (I like tons of garlic; you can back this off.)

6 big leaves of fresh basil, chopped

3 tablespoons of olive oil

½ teaspoon of salt

¼ teaspoon of freshly ground pepper

1 (2¼ oz.) can of sliced ripe olives, drained

1 cup of crumbled feta cheese

DIRECTIONS

1. The above measurements are good starters, but feel free to add more or less to taste. Cook pasta according to package directions. (If you're really feeling inspired, make your own pasta. All you need is semolina flour, eggs, and olive oil. You can find a recipe anywhere online. OK, if this is too much, just buy it from the store.)

2. While the pasta water is boiling, combine tomatoes and the next 5 ingredients. Salt the mixture and let the tomatoes soak up the salt for a few minutes; this will bring out the flavor of the tomatoes. (If heirloom tomatoes are in season, they work great.) Drain pasta and place in a large bowl.

3. Top with tomato mixture and sprinkle with olives and cheese.

Turn to pages 184–187 for appetizer, side, and dessert ideas that go well with this dish.

SPICED RED LENTIL DIP

*I'm always looking for a good appetizer that's unique but still delicious.
Once again, kudos to Regina for coming up with this one. Paired with
bread, veggies, or the perfect cracker, this is a beauty.* (SERVES 6–8)

INGREDIENTS

1½ cup of cooked lentils, drained
½ teaspoon of cumin
½ teaspoon of coriander
1 garlic clove, crushed
1½ tablespoons of lemon juice
1½ tablespoons of olive oil
Salt and pepper
Toasted pita to serve

DIRECTIONS

1. Place the lentils in a food processor and add cumin, coriander, garlic, lemon juice, salt and pepper to taste. Process to combine. Serve with bread.

MOM'S CORNBREAD

A solid accompaniment to the Southwest Chicken Soup or your favorite chili recipe.
(SERVES 6–8, DOUBLE RECIPE FOR A 9"X13" PAN)

INGREDIENTS

1 cup of self-rising corn meal
¾ cup of milk
1 egg
1 tablespoon of oil

DIRECTIONS

1. Preheat the oven to 400°.

2. Stir ingredients together in a mixing bowl. Pour into a greased 8"x8" pan and bake at 400° for 20 minutes or until brown.

SUMMER GAZPACHO

My mom has been making this recently and is trying to get me to embrace cold soup.
I have a problem with this. She said, "Don't think of it as cold soup; think of it as
a soupy salad." This actually didn't help. But everyone absolutely loves it, and it's
refreshing in the summer. (SERVES 6)

INGREDIENTS

1 garlic clove, minced

1 small onion, diced (I use sweet onion)

1 cucumber, peeled, seeded, diced

1 green pepper, diced

3 medium tomatoes, peeled but don't take out seeds. Dice. (I cut an X at the top and put it in boiling water for a minute or two, and the peel slides right off)

1 can of beef bouillon (or Better Than Bouillon®)

⅛ teaspoon of cayenne pepper

1 teaspoon of salt or to taste

4 tablespoons of lemon juice (fresh is always best)

¼ cup of red wine vinegar

¼ cup of vegetable oil (olive oil hardens in the fridge)

1½ tablespoons of dill

1 teaspoon of Worcestershire sauce

2½ cups of tomato juice

DIRECTIONS

1. Mix all ingredients into bite-size pieces. A food processor works best.

2. Refrigerate in a sealed container until chilled (approximately 3 to 4 hours).

3. Serve the soup cold, topped with desired garnishes.

BANOFFEE PIE

This dessert originated in England at a restaurant called The Hungry Monk. I ate there once, and this was perhaps the best dessert I've ever had. It's too good not to include in this new edition of Ruth. (SERVES 6–8)

INGREDIENTS

1½ cups of graham cracker crumbs
10 tablespoons of butter, melted
2 14-oz. cans of sweetened condensed milk
3 large bananas
1½ cups of heavy whipping cream

⅓ cup of confectioners' sugar
1 teaspoon vanilla
½ teaspoon of powdered instant coffee
Freshly ground coffee or chocolate shavings

DIRECTIONS

1. Mix graham cracker crumbs with melted butter and press the mixture into a 9" pie plate. Bake for 5 to 8 minutes. Allow to cool.

2. Immerse the unopened cans of sweetened condensed milk in a deep pan of boiling water. Cover and boil for 3 hours, making sure the cans remain covered with water. (Add water as needed.) Remove the cans from the water; allow them to cool completely before opening.*

3. Whip the cream with the sugar, vanilla, and instant coffee until thick and smooth. Spread 1/3 of the toffee over the base of the crust. Slice the bananas and lay them on the toffee. Spoon another 1/3 of toffee over the bananas. Layer more bananas and more toffee. Finally, spoon or pipe on the cream and lightly sprinkle with the freshly ground coffee or chocolate shavings.

Note: Boiling condensed milk in the can carries some risk. Alternatively, you can buy canned dulce de leche at the store.

CHOCOLATE POTS DE CRÈME

I am in love with light and airy desserts that are also made of chocolate. This dish is another Regina Pinto favorite of mine. She's delivered up a gem here. (SERVES 4)

INGREDIENTS

6 oz. of semisweet chocolate, chopped
2 cups of heavy cream
4 egg yolks
(If you'd like it sweeter, add 1 tablespoon
to ¼ cup of sugar)

FOR ASSEMBLING

Fruit of your preference
Whipped cream

DIRECTIONS

1. Preheat the oven to 400°.

2. In a saucepan, mix the chocolate and cream, stirring until melted and smooth. Bring to a boil. Let it cool slightly.

3. Place egg yolks in a large bowl and whisk until just mixed. If desired, add 1 tablespoon to 1/4 cup of sugar. Slowly add the chocolate mixture, whisking constantly until well mixed.

4. Put a dish towel on the bottom of a roasting pan. Divide the chocolate mixture between 4 individual ramekins. Fill the roasting pan halfway with water, covering the dish towel to keep the ramekins from sliding. Bake until a thin skin forms on top, approximately 10–20 minutes.

5. Remove the ramekins from the roasting pan and refrigerate until firm (minimum 1 hour).

6. Serve with a dollop of whipped cream and some raspberries or a fruit of your preference.

THE GREATER STORY OF REDEMPTION

WITH A PROPER BEGINNING, soaring plot, and epic ending, a well-written story is satisfyingly self-sufficient. This is certainly true of the book of Ruth, yet it does more than stand on its own. As we've seen, it's part of God's bigger story. And as the ending genealogy reveals, the book goes beyond the personal ventures of Ruth, Naomi, and Boaz; it foreshadows our own redemption through Jesus Christ. He is our ultimate Kinsman-Redeemer, the One who came to save us from our own versions of Moab.

Moab represents the place of our own choosing, where we live independent of God and on our own terms. Perhaps you have fared better than me, but I have made a terrible savior for myself. And where I have turned to people, possessions, career paths, and entertainment for help, I've been left disappointed and deserted. In the worst cases, I've found myself in a web of misery I didn't know how to get out of. I needed a Rescuer.

As Ruth was ostracized because of her race, and Naomi destitute because of her loss, they too needed rescue. In many respects, Boaz laid down his life for both Ruth and Naomi, risking the future of his estate and legacy for the certainty of theirs. But even the kinsman-redeemer Boaz needed a Redeemer greater than himself. It is to this Savior that the book of Ruth points.

The author of Luke put it plainly—Jesus came to seek and to save the lost (Luke 19:10). Paul said that while we were still sinners Jesus proved His love for us (Rom. 5:8).

First John 4:10 tells us, "This is love: not that we loved God, but that he loved us and *sent his Son* as an atoning sacrifice for our sins" (NIV, emphasis mine). The authors of the New Testament declare to us in vivid detail what Ruth had only hinted at: A Savior, Jesus Christ, who has come to save us from our sins.

Someone had to bear the natural consequences of our turning our backs on God. Instead of us bearing those consequences in endless separation from our Creator, the perfect Son of God stepped into our world and bore it for us. And after He died for our sin, He was raised from the dead so we could be saved by His life (Rom. 5:10). Never has a Redeemer been closer.

Dear one, He sees you, has sought you out, and given His very life for you. He's invited you to His table. My prayer is that you will revel in the linens of forgiveness that Jesus freely gives and that you will receive His invitation to enjoy abundant and forever life, which is to know Him, the only true God (John 17:3).

If you have never come to Jesus Christ to save you, may today be that glory-filled day.

Dearest Jesus, I need rescue. I need forgiveness for my sin so that I might be restored to relationship with You. I thank You that You didn't merely risk Your estate, but You left ultimate peace and fulfillment in heaven, dwelt among us, died on a cross while taking the punishment that should have been mine, and were resurrected, all so I could be restored to relationship with You.

There is no Redeemer like Jesus.

ENDNOTES

Session Two

1. D. I. Block, *Judges, Ruth,* Vol. 6 (Nashville: Broadman & Holman Publishers, 1999), 627.

2. Matthew Henry, *Matthew Henry's Commentary on the Whole Bible: Complete and Unabridged in One Volume* (Peabody: Hendrickson, 1994), 373.

3. Block, 605.

4. Robert L. Hubbard, *The Book of Ruth* (Grand Rapids, MI: William B. Eerdmans Publishing Company, 1988), 104.

5. Iain M. Duguid, *Esther and Ruth* (Phillipsburg, NJ: P&R Publishing Co., 2005), 163.

6. Warren W. Wiersbe, *The Bible Exposition Commentary*: The Complete *Old Testament in One Volume* (Colorado Springs: David C. Cook, 2007), 479–480.

Session Three

1. *The Wizard of Oz,* directed by Victor Fleming, Metro-Goldwyn-Mayer (MGM), 1939.

2. Ibid.

3. Hubbard, 123.

4. W. Baker and E. E. Carpenter, *The Complete Word Study Dictionary: Old Testament* (Chattanooga, TN: AMG Publishers), 740.

5. Tim Keller, *Genesis Study: What were we put in the world to do?* (Redeemer Presbyterian Church, 2006), 39.

6. Ibid.

7. Hubbard, 131.

8. *Psalms through Song of Songs*, Vol. 5, ed. T. Longman III (Barbour Publishing, 2010), 102.

9. Block, 651.

10. Ibid.

11. Ibid., 653.

12. Elizabeth Barrett Browning, *Aurora Leigh* (London: J. Miller, 1864; reprinted: Chicago: Academy Chicago Printers, 1979), https://digital.library.upenn.edu/women/barrett/aurora/aurora.html.

13. Knut Heim, "How and Why We Should Read the Poetry of the Old Testament for Public Life Today," Comment, November 14, 2011, https://comment.org/how-and-why-we-should-read-the-poetry-of-the-old-testament-for-public-life-today/.

14. Ibid.

15. Hubbard, 146.

16. Ibid., 160.

17. Block, 660.

18. Ibid.

19. Ibid., 659.

Session Four

1. Hubbard, 163.

2. Ibid.

3. Block, 661.

4. Hubbard, 169.

5. Block, 665.

6. Block, 666.

7. Ibid.

8. Ibid., 667.

9. Hubbard, 173–174.

10. Block, 670.

11. Ibid., 670–671.

12. Hubbard, 188–190.

13. Block, 674.

14. Ibid., 675.

15. Ibid.

16. Ibid., 674.

Session Five

1. Block, 683.

2. Hubbard, 201, 218.

3. Block, 687.

4. Block, 687–688.

5. Block, 684.

6. "Joshua, Judges, Ruth," *Ancient Christian Commentary on Scripture*, ed. John R. Franke (Downers Grove, IL: InterVarsity Press, 2005), 187.

7. Block, 690.

8. Block, 693.

9. A. E. Cundall and L. Morris, *Judges and Ruth: An Introduction and Commentary*, Vol. 7 (Downers Grove, IL: InterVarsity Press, 196), 281.

10. Duguid, 173.

11. Block, 700.

12. Ibid.

Session Six

1. Cundall and Morris, 289.

2. Block, 708.

3. Cundall and Morris, 288.

4. Lucy Maud Montgomery, *The Anne of Green Gables Collection* (Read Books Ltd., 1909, 2017).

5. Duguid, 182.

6. P. Cassell, as quoted by Cundall and Morris, 289.

7. Block, 720.

8. Ibid.

9. Hubbard, 256–257.

10. Hubbard, 257.

11. Hubbard, 258.

12. Hubbard, 256.

13. Cundall and Morris, 301.

14. Hubbard, 267.

Session Seven

1. Block, 731.

2. Hubbard, 274–276.

3. Block, 730.

4. Block, 732.

5. Hubbard, 272.

6. Block, 724.

7. Block, 736.

STUDIES FROM KELLY MINTER

ENCOUNTERING GOD
Cultivating Habits of Faith Through the Spiritual Disciplines
7 sessions

Unpack the biblical foundation for spiritual disciplines, including ways to practice disciplines like prayer, study, worship, rest, simplicity, generosity, celebration, and more.

lifeway.com/encounteringgod

ALL THINGS NEW
A Study on 2 Corinthians
8 sessions

Study the letter of 2 Corinthians to discover how God can use you no matter your situation.

lifeway.com/allthingsnew

FINDING GOD FAITHFUL
A Study on the Life of Joseph
8 sessions

Trace the path of Joseph's life in the book of Genesis to observe how God's sovereignty reigns, even in our darkest moments.

lifeway.com/findinggodfaithful

WHAT LOVE IS
The Letters of 1, 2, 3 John
7 sessions

Delve into the letters of 1, 2, and 3 John, written to encourage followers of Jesus to remain faithful to the truth. Glimpse not only the heart of John but also the heart of Jesus.

lifeway.com/whatloveis

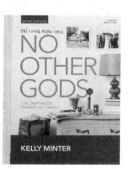

NO OTHER GODS
The Unrivaled Pursuit of Christ
8 sessions

Learn to identify the functional gods you may unknowingly be serving to experience the abundant life only Jesus can give.

lifeway.com/noothergods

NEHEMIAH
A Heart That Can Break
7 sessions

Nehemiah's heart was so broken for those in need that he left the comfort of his Persian palace to help them. Are you ready to let God break your heart for a hurting, lost world and move you to be the hands and feet of Jesus?

lifeway.com/nehemiah

lifeway.com/kellyminter | 800.458.2772

Lifeway women

Pricing and availability subject to change without notice.

Will you join Kelly

IN CARING FOR THE POOR, THE ORPHANED & THE FORGOTTEN?

Justice & mercy
INTERNATIONAL

Justice & Mercy International (JMI) is a Christ-centered, non-profit organization that cares for the vulnerable and forgotten in the Amazon and Moldova. Join Kelly Minter, our long-time mission partner, in making a difference with JMI. **Scan the QR code** below or visit *justiceandmercy.org/cultivate* for more information.

Connect WITH JMI

Follow us on social media to keep up with the work of JMI.

f ⊙ *@JusticeAndMercyInt* 🐦 *@JusticeMercyInt*

Get the most from your study.

DVD set, includes 7 video teaching sessions from Kelly Minter, each approximately 30–35 minutes

IN THIS STUDY, YOU'LL:

- Understand how God's law was and is meant to lead to life and flourishing for His people.
- Learn to trust God's providence even when redemption in your circumstances may seem impossible.
- Trace shadows of Jesus, the Messiah to come, in Ruth's story.

To enrich your study experience, consider the accompanying video teaching sessions, approximately 30–35 minutes, from Kelly Minter.

STUDYING ON YOUR OWN?

Watch Kelly Minter's teaching sessions, available via redemption code for individual video-streaming access, printed in this Bible study book.

LEADING A GROUP?

Each group member will need a *Ruth* Bible Study Book, which includes video access. Because all participants will have access to the video content, you can choose to watch the videos outside of your group meeting if desired. Or, if you're watching together and someone misses a group meeting, she'll have the flexibility to catch up! A DVD set is also available to purchase separately if desired. Visit **lifeway.com/ruth** for free leader resources.

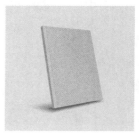

Teen girls' Bible study book, 7-session study

Browse study formats, a free session sample, video clips, church promotional materials, and more at

lifeway.com/ruth

Here's Your Video Access.

To stream *Ruth* Bible study video teaching sessions, follow these steps:

1. Go to my.lifeway.com/redeem and register or log in to your Lifeway account.

2. Enter this redemption code to gain access to your individual-use video license:

Once you've entered your personal redemption code, you can stream the video teaching sessions any time from your Digital Media page on my.lifeway.com or watch them via the Lifeway On Demand app on any TV or mobile device via your Lifeway account.

There's no need to enter your code more than once! To watch your streaming videos, just log in to your Lifeway account at my.lifeway.com or watch using the Lifeway On Demand app.

QUESTIONS? WE HAVE ANSWERS!

Visit support.lifeway.com and search "Video Redemption Code" or call our Tech Support Team at 866.627.8553.

This video access code entitles you to one non-transferable, single-seat license with no expiration date. Please do not share your code with others. Videos are subject to expiration at the discretion of the publisher. Do not post Bible study videos to YouTube, Vimeo, any social media channel, or other online services for any purpose. Such posting constitutes copyright infringement and is prohibited by the terms of use. Unauthorized posting also violates the service rules, which can negatively affect your YouTube or other service account.